BRIGHT NOTES

THE RED BADGE OF COURAGE BY STEPHEN CRANE

Intelligent Education

Nashville, Tennessee

BRIGHT NOTES: The Red Badge of Courage
www.BrightNotes.com

No part of this publication may be used or reproduced in any manner whatsoever without written permission, except in the case of brief quotations in critical articles and reviews. For permissions, contact Influence Publishers http://www.influencepublishers.com.

ISBN: 978-1-645424-06-2 (Paperback)
ISBN: 978-1-645424-07-9 (eBook)

Published in accordance with the U.S. Copyright Office Orphan Works and Mass Digitization report of the register of copyrights, June 2015.

Originally published by Monarch Press.
Joseph E. Grennen; W. John Campbell, 1965
2019 Edition published by Influence Publishers.

Interior design by Lapiz Digital Services. Cover Design by Thinkpen Designs.

Printed in the United States of America.

Library of Congress Cataloging-in-Publication Data forthcoming.
Names: Intelligent Education
Title: BRIGHT NOTES: The Red Badge of Courage
Subject: STU004000 STUDY AIDS / Book Notes

CONTENTS

1) Introduction to Stephen Crane   1

2) Brief Summary   5

3) Textual Analysis
   - Chapters 1 and 2   12
   - Chapters 3-5   31
   - Chapters 6-11   48
   - Chapters 12-17   69
   - Chapters 18-24   84

4) Character Analyses   99

5) Critical Commentary   103

6) Essay Questions And Answers   108

7) Topics For Research And Critical Analysis   113

8) Guide to Further Study   115

9) Bibliography   119

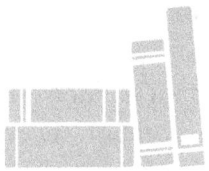

INTRODUCTION TO STEPHEN CRANE

THE LIFE OF STEPHEN CRANE

Stephen Crane was born in Newark, New Jersey, November 1, 1871, the youngest of fourteen children. His father, a Methodist pastor, died in 1880, and the family, after moving about several times, finally settled in Asbury Park, New Jersey, in 1882. In 1888 young Crane gained experience in reporting local events for his brother's news bureau and then later in the year went to Claverack College. After two years at Claverack, Crane went in 1890 to Lafayette College and in the spring of 1891 to Syracuse University, staying only one semester at each school, where his propensity for baseball seems to have outweighed his prowess as a student. It was while he was at Syracuse, however, that he composed the first draft of *Maggie: A Girl of the Streets*, a lengthier version of which he published under a nom de plume (and at his own expense) in 1893. In the summer of 1891 Crane made the closer acquaintance of the noted American writer Hamlin Garland (they had met before), from whom he received great encouragement (especially for the completed story later to be called *The Red Badge of Courage*). Then for over two years, the aspiring author plodded along doing journalistic work, trying all the time to place his manuscript of *The Red Badge*. Finally, in 1894, it appeared serially in the *Philadelphia Press*; the next year - in October - it was published in book form (appearing about two months later in a London edition). It was the book's generally enthusiastic reception by English readers which established Crane's reputation. Also appearing in 1895 was a volume of his verse, *The Black Riders*, to be followed by *George's Mother* and a new edition of *Maggie: A Girl of the Streets* in 1896.

From 1896 until his death in 1900 Crane kept a residence in England, though in 1896 he went as a correspondent for New York papers on a filibustering expedition to Cuba, on which, it is generally believed, he contracted the illness that was eventually to end his life. From his actual experience, however, he produced the fine story *The Open Boat* (published in 1898 in *The Open Boat and Other Tales of Adventure*). After Cuba, he traveled to Greece to report the Greco-Turkish war, and while there married Cora Taylor. In 1899 appeared another volume of poems, *War Is Kind*, as well as *Active Service: A Novel* and *The Monster and Other Stories*. In constant ill health all this while, Crane eventually traveled to the health spa at Badenweiler, Germany, where he met his death on June 5, 1900.

A number of his works were published after his death, and in 1925-7 appeared the monumental *The Work of Stephen Crane*, in twelve volumes edited by Wilson Follett. Since that time critical and scholarly interest in Crane has increased, until today he has achieved the status of a minor classic.

WORKS OTHER THAN THE RED BADGE OF COURAGE

Crane wrote a number of war stories, of which *The Red Badge* is the supreme example, but he also achieved notable successes with his naturalistic stories of life in New York City (*Bowery Tales*), his Western stories, and his tales based on his experiences as a war reporter.

BOWERY TALES

Crane's outstanding accomplishment in this vein is *Maggie: A Girl of the Streets*. It concerns the life of a young girl brought up in a "Hell's kitchen" in New York by alcoholic parents (the father dies early in the story; the mother becomes a notorious drunkard and jailbird). Poverty, ignorance, and a loveless family life in squalid surroundings absolutely condition Maggie to be the victim of the first man who offers a chance of release. He is Pete, a friend of her brother Jimmy, and she mistakes his blandishments (he is actually a gross, callous, and fatuous individual - the product of a similar upbringing) for love and loyalty. He "ruins" Maggie and deserts her for a more attractive woman. Her mother and brother (as well as the neighbors) in their ignorance assume an air of puritanical self-righteousness and spurn Maggie's attempt to return home. Her only alternative (as Crane presents it) is to become a streetwalker.

After some time, Maggie dies, and her remorseful family hold a wake during which they vacillate between emotion-filled recollections of a better time and Bowery mission cliches. The tale ends with the mother ironically acceding to the pleas of a mourning hypocrite to "forgive" her daughter.

TALES OF ADVENTURE

Some critics regard *The Open Boat* as Crane's finest achievement. Based on an actual incident, the story involves four shipwrecked men in a lifeboat: the cook, the oiler, the correspondent (Crane), and the captain (who is injured). Such action as there is - mainly a simple record of their gradual approach to land, continually opposed and thwarted by the raging waves and by darkness - is simply a background for a prolonged ironic reflection on nature's indifference (it may even be hostility) to man. The ironic narrator also comments bitterly on the failure of romantic attitudinizing about war and danger by comfortably situated aesthetes to represent adequately the harsh reality of suffering or even the basic nobility of unaccommodated man. Even the outcome of the action is an ambiguous matter. Three of the men reach land safely, but the oiler has drowned and faces only the "sinister hospitality of the grave."

STORIES OF THE AMERICAN WEST

The Bride Comes to Yellow Sky is easily the best of the Western stories. It opens with Jack Potter, the marshal of Yellow Sky, returning from San Antonio with his new bride. Not only does he display the traditional gaucheness of the newly married man, but he suffers a vague unrest at the thought of the reception they will receive in Yellow Sky; in some undefined way he has violated the frontier code. As the train pulls into town, the windows of the Weary Gentleman saloon are being boarded up, against the possible rampage of the town drunk and sometime badman Scratchy Wilson. The denizens of the saloon look to Jack Potter as their only salvation from Wilson. As Potter and his bride round a corner, they come face to face with Scratchy, who is nonplussed to discover that Potter is married and without a gun, and that a showdown is thus rendered impossible. Beneath the accidental fact of Potter's lack of a gun is the subtle realization by the two men that a border has been crossed - a way of life passed into history. The scene is one of Crane's most superb treatments of character involvement.

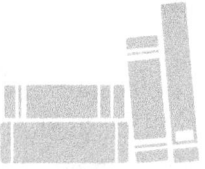

THE RED BADGE OF COURAGE

BRIEF SUMMARY

BEFORE THE BATTLE - CHAPTERS 1-3

As the book opens an army (identified only as the "soldiers in blue") is encamped on the banks of a river (unspecified, though it is apparently the Rappahannock since Crane seems to have modeled the forthcoming battle mainly on the Battle of Chancellorsville). A certain "tall soldier" reports to his comrades that they are going to move in behind the enemy on the next day, and all begin (in their ignorance) to debate the issue and trade opinions. A certain "youthful private" (later identified as Henry Fleming) retires to his bunk to reminisce about the romantic daydreams which had been partially the cause of his enlisting, and to speculate about his probable conduct in battle. The reactions of his mother and friends had been disappointingly prosaic, and his own thoughts, now vacillating between panic and reasoned assurance, finally develop into a determination to "accumulate information of himself" and to guard vigilantly against the prospect of being disgraced by facets of his being that he knows nothing of. He is encouraged to learn that even the "tall soldier" (now called Jim Conklin) does not possess an over-abundance of self-confidence either.

The next morning proves the rumor of the march to have been a mistake and the youth has further opportunity to consider himself and his comrades. He moves between the beliefs that they are all heroes, and all craven cowards, and he becomes more anxious for the battle which will settle these matters, even cursing the generals for their delay. Finally, the march begins and several incidents (a trivial conversation between a general and colonel, a soldier stepping on a comrade's hand, and a fat soldier trying to steal a horse) increase the youth's confusion about the nature of war and heroism, and as they camp for the night he begins to think self-pityingly of home when he is interrupted by a "loud soldier" (Wilson) whose braggadocio undermines the youth's confidence even further.

On the following night the regiment makes its bivouac further up river, and in the morning the men are routed out for a rapid march, during which they shed many unessential accouterments and then settle down in the forest for some days of waiting. One morning the youth awakens to find himself being carried along on a dead run, and finally realizes that he is being led to the slaughter. Passing groups of skirmishers and dead soldiers, the youth at first wishes to cry out a warning to his comrades that they are about to be sacrificed to the "red gods" of war - but then lapses into a resigned silence. They are forced to dig (and then to abandon) various entrenchments. The youth feels this to be intolerable, but Conklin accepts it all philosophically. Suddenly, the battle noise explodes before their eyes, and while the youth gazes in astonishment, Wilson's aplomb goes to pieces as (with a gesture of self-pity) he hands Henry a packet of letters, convinced that he is to die.

BATTLE AND FLIGHT - CHAPTERS 4-8

The brigade halts in a grove, amidst the screams of shells and showers of foliage. The lieutenant of the youth's company is wounded, and reacts by swearing "wondrously." To the youth it is a tableau of chaos-mobs of men rushing wildly, officers cursing, punching, and bawling, and veterans cracking grim jokes. Though the reserves are pale and quaking, the youth resolves to get a closer look at the "monster" they are to face.

Abruptly, they see the enemy charging toward them and the youth momentarily feels inspired by a common cause; he detects a "subtle battle brotherhood" which he cannot reject. But the war atmosphere turns this into a grim rage, and ultimately into a "battle sleep," through which all actions seem to him not heroic but merely idiotic. Many are wounded but the enemy is repulsed, and the reserves congratulate one another. As he regards the battle flag the old thrill returns. Nature seems to have been undisturbed by all this "devilment."

Imagining his trial to have been passed, the youth is in an ecstasy of self-satisfaction. But suddenly, incredibly, the enemy appears once more. Men groan and complain, while the youth, quivering like a "jaded horse" from exhaustion, and noticing others around dropping their weapons and running, runs "like a rabbit." There is no shame in his face. Mingling with others he moves to the rear, passing a battery of "precise gunners," and a general who looks like a "businessman." As the general gets a report that the reserves have held, he holds "a little carnival of joy on horseback."

The youth in his guilt begins to rationalize his action. He sees himself as the enlightened man, saving himself for a worthier encounter and begins to pity himself for the misunderstanding of his motives which will certainly ensue. But as he regards nature around him, he is content that the law of self-preservation is on his side. Reaching a chapel-like grove, Henry encounters a decaying corpse, with which he "exchanges a long look," and then flees in horror.

Passing on, he meets with more corpses and later with a crowd of blood - stained men streaming to the rear. One laughs hysterically; another carries on his face "an unholy mixture of merriment and agony; another (a "spectral soldier") has the "gray seal of death" on his face. A "tattered man" falls in with him, and innocently interrogating the youth about his wound, sees Henry slink away in confusion.

THE RETURN TO CAMP - CHAPTERS 9–15

Something in the appearance of the spectral soldier makes the youth start. Recognizing him as Jim Conklin, the youth can only cry out "Jim, Jim" incoherently. They march on together, Henry promising to care for him, while Conklin clings "babelike" to his arm. Moving with "mysterious purpose," he tears away from Henry's grasp, staggers his way towards a nearby field with the youth and the tattered man skulking behind, and finally halts "at the rendezvous," his chest heaving violently. He falls, then bounces a little way from the earth, and as the flap of his jacket opens, Henry notices that he has been wounded in the side.

The two men finally break away from the spot, and the tattered man now begins to bemoan his own wounds, though he retains enough strength to ask Henry where his wound is located. In vague anger and confusion the youth deserts his companion, realizing that chance is sure to bare his secret eventually.

Alone once more, the youth has time to consider the aches and hungers of his body. Though swaying and tottering, he stays in the vicinity of the battle, half hoping for a blue defeat which would vindicate him. Then he denounces himself for his selfishness and, finally convinced that the blue army is destined to win, tries to invent a tale with which to excuse himself.

Suddenly the blue warriors appear on the run, all their courage vanished, and Henry imagines briefly that he might rally them. But as he stands in the line of retreat and clutches a soldier's arm, the man hits him with his rifle butt. Henry falls, writhing and groaning. When at last he is able to rise he sees a jumble of men upon the field in the "blue haze of evening" and he hurries on, his head swollen with pain. A man with a "cheery voice" suddenly materializes out of nowhere and steers Henry firmly ahead, keeping up a friendly chatter about the events of the day's battle. As if with a magic wand he conducts the youth back to his regiment, clasps his hand firmly, and disappears.

Henry shamefacedly approaches the fire with his story of having been separated and is gratified to find that Wilson and Simpson receive him sympathetically - Wilson especially, who is now no longer the "loud soldier" but a chastened, humble man, from this point on called "the friend." He binds Henry's "wound," and gives him coffee and his own blanket. Henry falls soundly asleep and awakes in the morning to the sound of distant firing. Acting abusive toward Wilson, he is amazed to note his friend's new-found humility. The youth can not resist a feeling of superiority and condescension, especially when Wilson sheepishly asks for his packet of letters. Filled with his own good qualities, Henry pictures himself telling his war stories to young ladies at home.

THE FIRST CHARGE - CHAPTERS 16-20

The regiment now relieves a command that has been long under fire, but is soon forced to retreat. Criticism of the generals is rife, and Henry is loud in his condemnations until a soldier's sarcastic remarks convince him of his own ridiculousness and impose a sense of modesty on him. The few sallies of impatience he gives vent to are curtailed by Wilson's mollifying rejoinders or the savage-minded lieutenant's commands to keep silent.

At length, however, the youth's exasperation at the enemy's relentless pursuit turns to rage, and he becomes an automation, firing furiously. His comrades are awe-struck at his prowess and he basks in the plaudits of his officers. "He has slept, and, awakening, found himself a knight." During a brief respite Fleming and Wilson overhear an officer's reference to their regiment as a "bunch of mule-drivers," but then keep this knowledge to themselves and prepare for the next onslaught. With Fleming at their head the blue soldiers make a frenzied charge, only to falter and stop before they reach the enemy line. Their color sergeant is hit and Fleming and Wilson, seizing the flag, try to make a stand, but the regiment is "a machine run down" and they are forced to retreat. Now it is the gray army's turn to charge, but they too are driven back, an event which inspires the youth's regiment with renewed confidence.

THE FINAL CHARGE - CHAPTERS 21-24

Returning to their own lines they face not only the jeers of the veterans but the rebuff of the general, who rides up to deride the colonel (MacChesnay) for the blunder he has committed in not going a hundred feet farther. While others take the reproach to heart Henry reacts with smug tranquillity, satisfied with his own personal accomplishments. To add to his self-esteem he learns that he and Wilson have been singled out for commendation by the colonel.

When their time again comes, the emaciated regiment turns to the fray, with the youth now the color-bearer; they fight swiftly and savagely, though once more Henry gives in to a romantic vision (of his body lying torn on the battlefield - a mute reproach to his critics), but this is soon dispelled by the grim sight of wounded and powder-stained comrades. At the colonel's command they charge in "an insane fever of haste"; Henry himself is "dazzled by the tension of thought and muscle." Aiming for the enemy flag, he plunges like a demon with Wilson at his side. With a mad cry Wilson seizes the flag from the mortally wounded enemy color-bearer. In the rush they take four of the enemy prisoner.

Marching rearward after their minor success, Fleming counts his blessings. His shameful deed remains hidden - his glorious one open and apparent. Yet the specter of the tall soldier continues to haunt him, and his eyes seem opened to new ways. He despises the "brass and bombast of his earlier gospels," and feeling a "quiet manhood" in himself Henry looks ahead to visions of "soft and eternal peace."

THE RED BADGE OF COURAGE

TEXTUAL ANALYSIS

CHAPTERS 1 AND 2

CHAPTER 1

The opening chapter of *The Red Badge of Courage* begins with a striking variant version of a conventional literary "beginning," that of the reverie, or "welcome to Spring." The opening of Chaucer's *Canterbury Tales* is a famous example of a high rhetorical treatment of the motif, as is Surrey's poem, "Description of Spring, Wherein Each Thing Renews Save Only the Lover:"

The soote season that bud and bloom forth brings With green hath clad the hill and eke the vale, The nightingale with feathers new she sings, The turtle to her make hath told her tale ...

T. S. Eliot, in *The Waste Land*, alters the traditional **imagery** for ironic effect:

April is the cruelest month, breeding Lilacs out of the dead land, mixing Memory and desire, stirring Dull roots with spring rain ...

Crane's opening words, like Eliot's, invert the traditional attitude, for, while he is ostensibly speaking of the transition from dawn to day, his **imagery** suggests the green awakening of Spring and ironically equates the military reveille to the surging of some giant in the earth vivified by the returning sun: "The cold passed reluctantly from the earth, and the retiring fogs revealed an army stretched out on the hills, resting. As the landscape changed from brown to green, the army awakened, and began to tremble with eagerness at the noise of rumors. It cast its eyes upon the roads, which were growing from long troughs of liquid mud to proper thoroughfares. A river, amber-tinted in the shadow of its banks, purled at the army's feet ...." This personification is continued in the image of the enemy camp at night, which appears as a "red, eyelike gleam of hostile camp fires set in the low brows of distant hills." After this generalized and symbolic introduction, the scene is focused more sharply as the narrator reports the appearance of "a certain tall soldier" waving a shirt like a banner as he returns from a brook where he had gone to wash it. Actually, the narrator is far from being a disinterested recorder of fact, and we note here a certain flippant, even sarcastic tone in his remark that the tall soldier had "developed virtues and went resolutely to wash a shirt," that he "came flying back" from the brook with news of a move on the next day, was "swelled with a tale he had heard," had "adopted [an] important air," spoke pompously, and so forth.

| Comment

To define the narrator's tone of address with precision, and thus to establish his attitude toward the facts he reports is essential to the interpretation of all works of fiction - especially so of *The Red Badge of Courage*. A central critical problem in Crane criticism, in fact, is the attempt to determine his attitude at different points in the narrative toward nature, toward his main character, Henry Fleming, and toward such abstractions as "courage" and "war." Here, the narrator's somewhat supercilious attitude toward the tall soldier and his comrades is a first inkling of his later treatment of the **theme** of the puniness of individual determination in the face of the uncontrollable forces of nature and of institutions.

The following paragraph sees the tall solder smugly mapping out a campaign based upon the fragment of information he has come by, and the two score soldiers who had just been "hilariously" encouraging the dancing of a Negro teamster reduced to small arguing groups, an event which implies the sudden and random shifts of mood and intention characteristic of men herded together for the purpose of waging war. This paragraph ends on the impressionistic detail: "Smoke drifted lazily from a multitude of quaint chimneys."

Comment

Basically, the impressionist author attempts to record the scene as it has momentarily impressed him - that is, to record those details of color, shape, and arrangement which have stood out in his vision as most suggestive of the mood inspired in him. Here, the lazily drifting smoke is perhaps meant to suggest the languid emotions of the soldiers, and the "multitude of quaint chimneys" something of the unreal, fairy-tale atmosphere which war engenders.

Another private, with a smooth flushed face, loudly denounces the report as a "thunderin' lie," and nearly comes to blows over it with the tall soldier. The narrator next reports the reactions of a certain corporal, and by choosing a deliberately inflated style and vocabulary for him (far above the dialect we assume to be natural to him) achieves the ironic effect of a viewpoint which perceives the absurdity which underlies all individual human designs: "He had just put a costly board floor in his house, he said. During the early spring he refrained from adding extensively to the comfort of his environment because he had felt that the army might start on the march at any moment." This tone of ironic superiority is the narrator's most frequent device, especially in the first half of the book. He goes on to remark, for instance, that many of the men now engaged in a "spirited debate"; that one outlined the commanding general's plans in a "peculiarly lucid manner"; and that some "advocated other plans of campaign." This is followed by a report of their conversation with the tall soldier (now called "Jim"), in a dialect which is plainly meant to suggest their farmer origins.

Comment

This rapid alternation of colloquial dialogue with expository passages couched in a comparatively learned and abstract vocabulary is itself an aspect of the book's style, and thus an index to its meaning. The reader quickly perceives the disparity between the two types of discourse and takes it as a symbol of the disparity between ambition and realization in those same individuals.

Listening to the remarks of the tall soldier and the comments of his comrades was "a certain youthful private" (Henry Fleming, though we do not learn his name until later - his last name not until Chapter 12. He is most often referred to as "the youth"). The youth repairs to his hut and crawls through and "intricate hole" to the interior in order to mull over some "new thoughts" (perhaps suggestive of a descent into the unconscious, though the whole question of the extent to which *The Red Badge* may be submitted to analysis as a "psychological quest" is in need of further study. Other aspects of this **theme** will be dealt with as they arise). The youth lies down on a wide bunk, and we are given a description of the hut. Cracker boxes, grouped about the fireplace, serve as chairs. A magazine illustration hangs on the wall, as do three rifles on pegs. A folded tent serves as a roof, while the sun makes it glow a light yellow. Smoke curls from the fire, and the "flimsy chimney of clay and sticks made endless threats to set ablaze the whole establishment." The youth, in a "trance of astonishment," considers his situation in a reverie which verges from ultra-romantic **cliches** about marital glory on the one hand, to sanguine predictions about modern "civilized" strife on the other. He dwells upon the idea of battles as "great affairs," as "vague and bloody conflicts that had thrilled him with their sweep and fire," in which he played the role of protector with "eagle-eyed prowess." But he had long ago dismissed these visions as "crimson blotches" on the world's history, as distant as crowns and castles. "He had long despaired of witnessing a Greeklike struggle.... Secular and religious education had effaced the throat-grappling instinct, or else firm finance held in check the passions."

Comment

Both the suppressed desire to participate in heroic combats, and the glib sociological truisms are forms of romantic or idealistic attitudes which show the youth as immature. His attitudinizing, moreover, is indicated by the obviously "poetical" and rhythmical quality of these sentences. Note particularly the almost regular rhythm of the final clause, the **consonance** on the s, c, and f sounds (especially the **alliteration** in "firm finance"), the e **assonance** in "sec," "ed," "eff," "else," "held," and "check"

THE RED BADGE OF COURAGE

(most particularly, the careful sound balance between "sec" and "check"). This sentence is repeated verbatim several pages later.

The next paragraph is almost a tableau in words. War, as it existed in the stylized daydreams of the youth, was nothing but "tales of great movements ... marches, sieges, conflicts ... large pictures extravagant in color, lurid with breathless deeds." The youth's reverie becomes in effect a flashback, as the narrator now contrasts his grandiose vision with his mother's prosaic analysis of the matter. She had discouraged him, with contempt for his ardor and numerous reasons to prove his greater importance to the farm than to the army, but the newspapers, gossip, and his own imaginings had aroused him beyond recall. (Apparently with some sarcasm, the narrator notes that the youth's decision was aided by daily newspaper accounts of decisive victories.) In bed one night, he heard the church bells "as some enthusiast jerked the rope frantically" to report news of a battle, and the outcries of the people as they rejoiced made him "shiver in a prolonged ecstasy of excitement." The next morning he enlisted.

Comment

It is important to note that the decision to enlist is the immediate result of a compulsive nervous reaction (the "shiver of ecstasy"), itself provoked by an act which is so described as to suggest that it, too, has a compulsive quality ("some enthusiast jerked the rope frantically"). An enthusiast, strictly speaking, is one possessed by a god, and the clear implication here is that war (or the god of war) radiates impulses which actually stimulate behavior beyond the power of the individual will to control, at least the will which is sensitive enough to imaginative stimuli such as the "clangoring of the church bell." ("Clangor," in this context, recalls John Dryden's famous line on the power of music: "The trumpet's loud clangor excites us to arms.")

    Henry's announcement that he had enlisted was greeted by his mother's stoic reply, "The Lord's will be done," while she continued to milk the brindle cow (though the youth did observe two tears to fall from her eyes). She had disappointed him by saying nothing about "returning with his shield or on it." This, of course, is the command that Spartan mothers are alleged to have issued to their famous warrior sons as they set out for battle, but Henry's mother, doggedly peeling potatoes, is a far cry from the romantic image he has dimly anticipated. Telling him not to try and "lick the hull rebel army," and to "keep quiet an' do what they tell yeh," she sends him off with eight pairs of socks and a cup of blackberry jam. Her parting speech, a long catalog of the bad influences a young man will be exposed to in the army, makes Henry impatient and uneasy. His departure is attended by feelings partly of relief and partly of shame, while he watches her brown, tear - stained face as she knelt among the potato parings. He goes to bid farewell to his schoolmates and meets the same sort of ambiguous response to his heroic gesture. Henry, and some others who had enlisted, strutted about in the wave of privileges they enjoyed for the afternoon, but there is an uneasy note in the "vivacious fun" which a certain dark girl made at his martial spirit, offset only by the vision of another girl who (it seemed to him) "grew demure and sad at sight of his blue and brass," and who became flustered when he spied her watching his departure from a window. On the trip to Washington, the fanfare, attention, smiles, and compliments the regiment received had the youth believing he must really be a hero. The narrator now briefly disposes of several ensuing months by remarking that "after complicated journeying with many pauses, there had come months of monotonous life in a camp," and indicating the onset of disillusionment in the youth - he had previously thought of war as a constant series of death struggles, but found that he had actually had little to do but sit and try to keep warm. This inactivity merely brought him back to his earlier theory about the disappearance of Greeklike struggles, and "firm finance" holding in check the passions. "He had grown to regard himself merely as a part of a vast blue demonstration."

Comment

This idea of the army and its movements as a "blue demonstration" is a thought which recurs in the youth's mind a number of times throughout the book. It suggests the impersonal character of warfare, the machinelike process of a military campaign, and the purposeless - almost academic - relationship it appears to bear to the intentions of the individual will. Warfare comes to seem a perfunctory organization of color and form, a natural phenomenon not vastly different from the annual burgeoning of spring, which might in its turn almost be termed a "green demonstration."

The youth, amid all the drilling and reviewing, seemed to have no other purpose than to look out for his personal comfort. The only enemies he had seen were some pickets along a river bank, a "philosophical lot," who occasionally shot "reflectively" at the blue pickets. There was actually a jaunty current of good-humored badinage which passed back and forth between the two lines, such exchanges as a reproach by the blue soldiers for having been shot at, and a reply by the gray that their guns had exploded without their permission. The youth even got on rather friendly terms with one of them, a fact which made him rather regret war temporarily.

Comment

The fact that this is the American Civil War (though Crane, of course, never explicitly admits it) points up the antithesis between the official national "emotion" of hatred for the enemy and the potential counter emotion of friendship for the individual foe. There are reliable accounts from other sources (for example, A. G. Empey's *Over the Top*, a memoir of the First World War) of opposing forces engaging each other in lighthearted conversation and even calling temporary truces during which they exchanged visits. Thomas Hardy's poem, "The Man He Killed," is a memorable expression of the same sentiment:

Had he and I but met By some old ancient inn, We should have set us down to wet Right many a nipperkin! But ranged as infantry, And staring face to face, I shot at him as he at me, And killed him in his place ...

Encounters of this sort were balanced by the tales he heard from veterans about gray, relentless hordes sweeping along like Huns, or of eternally hungry men whose "red, live bones" stuck out through rents in their uniforms. But he realized that recruits were prey to veterans' horror stories, which were not to be trusted. At this point he began to analyze the question of his own courage - to prove to himself mathematically that he would never run from battle. A slight panic grew in his mind as he anticipated an actual battle, "contemplated the lurking menaces of the future," and he began to waver in his belief in his own stout heart. His law of life and his knowledge of himself would be of no avail in a crisis, he felt. He was an "unknown quantity"; he would have to "experiment" again, and "accumulate information" about himself lest he should act in a way to bring disgrace upon him.

Comment

Crane is perhaps suggesting, through the "mathematical" and "scientific" terms which the youth here employs in his introspection, that the question of courage will not submit itself to this sort of analysis; that as long as Henry approaches the performance of brave deeds through an abstract process of rationalization about "courage" he will fail to achieve them.

At this point the tall soldier and the loud soldier enter the hut (the tall soldier does this "dexterously" through the same "intricate hole" Henry has previously entered - perhaps an indication of his greater mastery of self - knowledge). They are arguing about the rumored move, and to the youth's question, "Going to be a battle, sure, is there, Jim?", the tall one replies in the affirmative with the air of a man "about to exhibit a battle for the benefit of his friends." (We see how easily a clear perception of the danger and horror is dispelled by the personal triumph of "being right" in the matter. But when asked how he thinks the regiment will perform, he replies, "Oh, they'll fight all right, I guess," upon which the narrator sarcastically intones, "He made a fine use of the third person.") Under the youth's prodding the tall soldier (Jim) gives his opinion about the probable bravery of the members of the regiment. It is a masterpiece of uncertainty and ambiguity. A few might run ... or the whole regiment might turn tail ... then again they might stay "and fight like fun" ... they'll fight "better than some if worse than others" ... most of them will "fight like sin" after they once get shooting - and so forth. When Henry, in a half-joking fashion, asks Jim if he ever thought he might run himself the loud soldier giggles nervously, while Jim answers by saying that he would probably run if others did, but that if everybody stood and fought, why then he would stand and fight, too. "Be jiminey, I would. I'll bet on it."

Comment

Jim's reply is hardly an example of supreme self-assurance. His uncertainty gratifies and reassures the youth, who had feared that all the untried men were confident of their future bravery. Furthermore, his speech points up the problem of collective versus individual action. "Everybody" is, after all, an abstraction. A rout and a charge both must begin in the determined act of a single individual.

SUMMARY

From the outset we are confronted by the book's basic method of description and **exposition** - a deliberate vagueness about names, places, and times (even the opposing armies are not identified); broad strokes of description, selected for impressionistic and symbolic effect; and a consistent detachment on the part of the narrator, which takes the form of an ironic objectivity toward all characters except the youth, into whose mind we gain a limited access. The effect is to render with concrete particularity (from within the scene) the welter of thoughts and emotions which is characteristic of men in training for a battle. In addition, the following observations about character, **theme**, and style are worthy of note:

1. Three of the main characters are introduced: Henry Fleming, Jim Conklin, and Wilson, though they are referred to most often merely as the youth, the tall soldier, and the loud soldier (the youth sometimes as Henry; Wilson's name is not yet mentioned).

2. The primary issue in the book - the youth's dilemma over courage and cowardice - is presented in the form of self-analysis as well as dialogue with the tall soldier. He arrives at the point of being satisfied that his own uncertainties are typical of the rest of the untried men.

3. Sentence structure in general tends to be simple and uncomplicated, reflecting Crane's attempt to render reality with blunt objectivity. There is, however, a discernible undercurrent of more involved rhetorical structures, generally for ironic effect.

4. The author makes a marked use of color **imagery** (red, for instance, for **allusions** to war, glory, derring - do, etc.; yellow for the pall cast on romantic notions by mundane actualities such as the mother's discouraging reaction). **Metaphor**, and especially personification, is used frequently to suggest a kind of immanent will in nature itself (for example, "the chimney ... made endless threats to set ablaze the whole establishment").

5. There are frequent **allusions** to the trappings and motifs of the heroic ages (Greeklike struggles, the Spartan mothers, the horde of the Huns), which contribute to a pattern of ironic contrast between the youth's initial idealism and his growing disillusionment.

6. Vocabulary: the narrator often resorts to an elevated vocabulary to call attention to ironic contrast - that, for example, between the mother's deep moral rectitude and the effect the banality of her expression has on Henry's idealism: "Moreover, on her side, was his belief that her ethical motive in the argument was impregnable."

7. **"Poeticism"**: Crane occasionally slips into a markedly rhythmical form of expression, characterized by a high degree of sound patterning (such as **alliteration**) and colorful language, usually as an accompaniment to some high - flown sentiment. The effect is normally felt as **irony**. For instance: "He could not accept with assurance an omen that he was about to mingle in one of those great affairs of the earth."

CHAPTER 2

The next morning revealed that the tall soldier had been mistaken about the move. Scoffed at and sneered at, he had to defend his reputation by beating one of his detractors in a fistfight. This is no way solved the youth's problem. His self-questioning had to be postponed, as he resumed once more his "blue demonstration" theory. Days of "ceaseless calculations" proved nothing. He decided he would have to enter the "blaze" and make an objective consideration of the way his body behaved. Mental arithmetic would have to give way to a kind of chemical analysis - blaze, blood, and danger being, in effect, the chemist's precipitating acids. Even so, he tried "to measure himself" by his comrades, particularly by the tall soldier, a man he had known since early youth. How could Jim Conklin accomplish anything that Henry Fleming was incapable of doing? Perhaps Conklin had a false opinion of himself - on the other hand, perhaps he was indeed destined to achieve glory in combat.

Comment

There is a glancing, partial illumination in the youth's conclusion that only blaze, blood, and danger can give him the answer he seeks. (It is also an unwitting bit of prophecy.) Even his preference for a chemical rather than an arithmetic **metaphor** is something of an improvement in personal insight, though he still continues to "calculate," "measure," and "fathom" the depths of his problem.

The youth hoped to discover a comrade who had the same doubts as he, and tried to lure others into a confession of similar misgivings. He failed to do so. Moreover, he feared to tell his secret to anyone lest he prove to be an unworthy confidant, thus leaving himself open to derision. As for his companions, he alternated between two opinions, sometimes believing them all to be heroes, men of superior qualities who wore their courage without ostentation, at other times comforting himself in the belief that secretly they were all as terrified as he. Outwardly, they took the prospect of battle lightly, and he suspected that they might be liars. For these thoughts, however, he reproached himself as a sinner against the "gods of traditions."

The slowness of the generals seemed to him intolerable. They had no conception of his great problem, and his anger occasionally caused him to grumble about like a veteran. One morning, however, before daybreak, whispered rumors caused some uneasiness in the ranks. Against a yellow patch in the sky (which looked like a rug laid for the coming sun) was silhouetted the figure of the colonel on his horse. Vague tramplings and mysterious shadows added to the youth's impatience. Suddenly the "mystic gloom" was pierced by battle sounds, and he saw the colonel calmly stroking his mustache. Suddenly he heard the clatter - the "clickety-click" - of a horse's hooves, and a jangling rider appeared to deliver a message to the colonel. As he rode off he shouted back (to the youth's astonishment), "Don't forget that box of cigars."

Comment

The youth is mystified because, in his inexperience, he cannot comprehend the casual attitude of the professional soldier toward what to him is an encounter charged with romance, mystery, and extraordinary personal involvement.

As the regiment moved off it resembled a monster "wending with many feet." (Crane's choice of the archaic verb "wend" [meaning "walk," with the additional **connotation** of "turning"] reinforces in a minor way the motif of fairy-tale unreality.) The men stumbled along, muttering and arguing, until one fell down and another stepped on his hand. In a brief **parody** of the style of **epic** "naming" the narrator refers to him as "he of the injured fingers," and reports that he swore bitterly, to which the rest responded with nervous laughter. As they strode along, a "dark regiment" in front of them and a "tinkle of equipment" behind came to be seen in the rising dawn as two thin, black lines disappearing over a hill before them and into a wood behind. They resembled "two serpents crawling from the cavern of the night." The river, however, was nowhere in sight, so that the tall soldier (the narrator remarks) "burst into praises of what he thought to be his powers of perception."

Comment

Here again we notice the deliberate rhetoric of an elevated vocabulary and alliterative phrasing being used to comment ironically on the self-deluding pomposity of certain characters.

Some agree with Jim Conklin; some offer other theories. But the youth continues in his own "eternal debate." He becomes gloomy and suspicious, looking anxiously ahead for signs of combat. He sees nothing but a dun - colored cloud of smoke floating in a sky of fairy blue, and is disappointed to see not a melancholy aspect like his own but a gleeful look on the faces of the others in his regiment. They spoke with assurance of victory, "felicitating themselves upon being a part of a blasting host."

Comment

The strong suggestion of the idea of "blight" (in the word "blast" - compare, for instance, John Milton's "O fairest flower, no sooner blown but blasted") is perhaps the faint beginning of a pattern of flowery **imagery** Crane employs to convey the sense of war as outrageous floral growth - a satanic form of nature - on the earth's face. It is ironic that the regiment here congratulates itself on "blasting" the enemy, but will soon pitch camp and "sprout" wildly. "Tents sprang up," says the narrator, "like strange plants. Camp fires, like red, peculiar blossoms, dotted the night."

It is here that the youth's sense of isolation intensifies. As the rest rejoice on being "part of host," and laugh merrily at the company wags even to the point of forgetting their mission, the youth is saddened by their blithe demeanor. "Whole brigades grinned in unison, and regiments laughed," but his separation becomes more total. In counterpoint to his growing seriousness the regiment as a whole begins to treat the entire affair as a lark - a schoolboy escapade. A fat soldier attempts to steal a horse from a dooryard but is routed by a young girl, and the regiment whoops and enter "whole-souled upon the side of the maiden." They jeer at the private and give the girl enthusiastic support. When they pitch camp that night the youth keeps to himself, and wanders into the gloom. The numerous fires, we are told, "with the black forms of men passing to and fro before the crimson rays, made weird and satanic effects." As he lay in the grass, enveloped by night and caressed by winds, he felt a "vast pity" for himself and imagined that the surrounding mood was that of an encompassing sympathy for him.

Henry reflects on his life at home, and wishes that despite the tedious round of tasks in barn and house he could be back there once again. In his present vision the brindle cow and her mates each have a "halo of happiness" about their heads, and he would have given anything to return to them and put a great distance between himself and those men who were now "dodging implike around the fires."

Comment

The "implike" men and the "weird and satanic effects" they produce are certainly meant to suggest the devotees of an unholy creed, just as the "halo of happiness" about the cows' heads is a whimsical suggestion of farm duties as a form of "religion." It is important for the reader to notice even the casual manifestations of the religious **metaphor** Crane brings into play if he wishes to respond properly to the representation of Jim Conklin's death in Chapter 9. (Just before Jim falls, for instance, he is seen in the grip of "implike enthusiasm.")

Suddenly the loud soldier (Wilson) approached, and began to speak in an optimistic way of their chances in the coming battle. Gleeful and exultant, he exclaims "this time - we'll lick'em good!" His face is described as boyish, he walks with an elastic step, and he speaks with youthful enthusiasm: "Gee rod! how we will thump 'em!" His pride and boisterous anticipation of success provoke only bitter sarcasm from Henry, who asks how he can be sure he will not run, and follows up Wilson's denial with a reminder that many good men have run from battle in the past. He finally stirs Wilson to the angry rejoinder, "Who are you, anyhow? You talk as if you thought you was Napoleon Bonaparte."

Failing to discover a sympathetic chord in Wilson, he becomes more wretched than before, and goes to his tent, where he falls asleep by the side of the tall soldier. Fear takes the form in his mind of a thousand-tongued monster he could never hope to cope with, even though others might go about the business of war with absolute coolness. He sweats in anguish at these visions, while the voices of his comrades, who are calmly gambling nearby, float to him on the night air. The youth stares at the "red, shivering reflection of a fire" on the wall of his tent until he falls asleep.

SUMMARY

There is very little action in Chapter 2. The first dozen paragraphs show the regiment encamped for an unspecified period of time, during which the youth has time to consider his problem at length. Then the regiment advances up the bank of the river; a man falls and injures his hand; a fat soldier tries unsuccessfully to steal a horse; and, finally, the regiment pitches camp for the night. Additional points:

1. The youth, in trying to forecast his reactions in battle, goes about it as a problem to be "calculated," though he has a dim intuition that an abstract solution of it is beyond him. He remains isolated in his spiritual suffering.

2. The religious **metaphor** is continued in such images as:

   a. the "mystic gloom" of morning with the colonel silhouetted against a yellow path of sky which almost resembles an oriental prayer rug.

   b. the weird, satanic effects created by implike shadows in the firelight.

3. There are a number of minor images which provide partial, ironic perspectives on a variety of human attitudes toward war:

   a. the tall soldier is called the "fast flying messenger of a mistake," as if he were some ignoble Hermes.

   b. some of the men talk excitedly about the battle "as of a drama they were about to witness."

   c. the youth tends to interpret distant figures as "monsters," "dragons," "reptiles," or "serpents," all images which convey his complicated sense of the horror and yet the romance of war.

THE RED BADGE OF COURAGE

TEXTUAL ANALYSIS

CHAPTERS 3-5

CHAPTER 3

On the next night the columns of marching men, looking like purple streaks, filed across a river, the waters of which appear wine-tinted by a glaring fire. (One of Homer's constant epithets for the sea in his Iliad is "the wine-dark sea.) The fire also caused occasional gleams of gold or silver among the troops, while out of the mysterious shadows cast by the hills of the farther shore came the "solemn" song of insects.

Comment The Impressionistic choice of details here ("purple streaks," "wine-tinted water," "gleams of gold," "solemn song" of insects, and so on) suggest strongly that the approach to battle is to be taken as a kind of dark, satanic sacrament, in which the marching columns have the aspect of a sacrificial offering, and thus continues the thread of "religious" imagery.

The youth, fearing an immediate assault, watched the woods carefully, but the regiment arrived at a camping place and its soldiers slept the brave sleep of wearied men.

Comment

"Brave sleep" is an excellent example of the vigor and freshness of Crane's language. It probably owes something to the famous **couplet** from William Collins' "Ode Written in the Year 1746,"

How sleep the brave, who sink to rest By all their country's wishes bless'd!

Yet, for Crane, it is not the men but the sleep which is "brave"; he thus questions ironically the very meaning of "bravery" (which, in fact, in earlier periods of the English language, meant "bravado," or even merely "insulting cheek").

In the morning they were aroused once more, and led further into the forest, losing as they marched many of the signs of a new command. Aching feet and perspiration led to grumblings. Knapsacks and thick shirts were shed. Soon only the most necessary equipment was being carried. "You can now eat and shoot," said the tall soldier, "that's all you want to do." (This divestiture of clothing, which certainly represents the increasing hold which nature is exerting over the soldiers, is not an uncommon form of literary symbolism. There are examples as diverse as Eugene O'Neill's *The Emperor Jones*, in which Jones' loss of his clothing accompanies a reversion to savagery - to the primitive roots of his psyche - and Shakespeare's *King Lear*, in which Lear's nakedness during the storm on the heath symbolizes unaccommodated man standing powerless before nature.) Even so, the narrator's attitude remains ambiguous, and he calls himself back from any possible hint of overseriousness with the comment, But there was much loss of valuable knapsacks, and, on the whole, very good shirts.

For all that, they did not yet look like veterans, and they had to put up with the jibes of returning warriors directed against their unspoiled ranks and the newness of their uniforms. Given a while to rest, the youth, moved by the odor of "peaceful pines," the monotony of ax blows, and the "crooning" of insects, returned to his theory of a "blue demonstration." Suddenly, early one morning, he was awakened by being kicked in the leg by the tall soldier, and found himself running down a road surrounded by other panting men. His canteen banged "rhythmically" on his thigh and his haversack "bobbed softly," while all around he could hear men whispering "jerky" sentences of complaint and reproach. (This is perhaps a suggestion of an opposition between the rhythm of instinctual motions and the relatively disordered pattern of analytical thought.) The damp fog and sudden spattering of firing bewildered him. He could not think, and merely felt himself carried along by a mob. The sun now spread "disclosing rays" and, one after another, "regiments burst into view like armed men just born of the earth."

Comment

This is unquestionably an **allusion** to the myth of Cadmus, who, as he prepared to sacrifice a cow to Athene, was set upon by the serpent which guarded the Castalian spring. The serpent having killed almost all of Cadmus' men, he crushed its head with a rock and (at Athene's command) sowed its teeth in the ground, whereupon armed men sprang up. Cadmus escaped by throwing a rock among them, causing a brawl in which nearly all were killed. To what extent the part played by cow and serpent in this myth may be related to Crane's symbolic use of the mother's brindle cows and his serpentine imagery is a question worthy of consideration.

    The youth felt that his moment had come. He was about to be measured, and he found himself in a "moving box" bound by the iron rules of tradition and law. He began to complain of his fate. He had been dragooned into the army by a merciless government, and now he was going to be slaughtered. The regiment moved across a little stream and climbed a hill on the opposite side, amid the boom of artillery. Quickly his fear gave way to curiosity, and he scrambled up the bank eagerly, expecting to find a battle scene. (Crane is not explicit at this point, but it is clear that the youth's romantic dreams have gotten the upper hand momentarily, and that he is swiftly disappointed by the prosaic scene of confusion which greets his eyes.) Some fields are squeezed in by a forest; there are "knots" of skirmishers running "hither and thither," and firing aimlessly. Other regiments "flounder" up the bank, as skirmishers continually "melt into the scene" only to reappear in other places. They were always "busy as bees," absorbed in their "little combat."

Comment

The phrase "busy as bees" (in its proverbial application at least as old as the sixteenth-century writer John Lyly's *Euphues*, which refers to "an old man, as busy as a bee") well illustrates the ironic extremes to which Crane's tone verges. On the one hand it has the absurd **connotations** of diminutiveness, perhaps mainly due to Isaac Watts' sentimental poem, How doth the little busy bee Improve each shining hour And gather honey all the day From every opening flower!

But it also suggests the analogy between the human and the bee communities, a matter which has long been the subject of serious investigation, and thus tends to define warfare as another instance of blind, instinctual forces.

The youth tried to avoid obstacles, but his "forgotten feet" knocked against stones or became entangled in thorns (another indication of a merging with nature itself). In short, instead of coming upon a tapestry depicting a heroic battle fought by dashing, splendidly dressed warriors, he became "aware that these battalions with their commotions were woven red and startling into the gentle fabric of softened greens and browns."

Once the youth encountered the body of a dead soldier, dressed in an awkward, yellowish suit, and worn shoes from which a dead foot "projected piteously." The ranks had to open to avoid the corpse. The youth peered vainly at the ashen face and tawny beard for an answer to his great Question. Now his ardor had faded and his curiosity was satisfied. (Crane now provides a short expository comment, which is an important key to the youth's later failure of nerve: "... If an intense scene had caught him with its wild swing as he came to the top of the bank, he might have gone roaring on. This advance upon Nature was too calm. He had an opportunity to reflect. He had time in which to wonder about himself and to attempt to probe his sensations."

Comment

Surely the comparison with Shakespeare's Prince Hamlet is an apt one here. In his failure to take decisive action, Hamlet soliloquizes:

Thus conscience does make cowards of us all; And thus the native hue of resolution Is sicklied o'er with the pale cast of thought, And enterprises of great pith and moment With this regard their currents turn awry, And lose the name of action.

Indeed, the question of whether the youth has acted as a "coward" has hardly more relevance to Crane's **theme** than the identical question as put to the actions of Hamlet, or even of Shakespeare's Falstaff (1 *Henry IV*). Crane is more concerned with such things as the relationship between native sensitivity and "crowd Psychology," or between feeling and thought as opportunity makes room for one or the other to dominate.

The landscape appeared to threaten him, a coldness crept over his back, and his legs seemed not to fit in his trousers at all. A distant house took on an ominous look. He doubted the competence of the generals, and imagined that they were all about to be sacrificed. He expected the "stealthy approach of death." The youth wanted to warn his comrades of the generals' idiocy - to step forth and make a "passionate speech." But the line of soldiers went calmly on, most of them wearing expressions of intense interest, appearing absorbed in what they were doing. They "were going to look at war, the red animal-war, the blood-swollen god. And they were deeply engrossed in this march." The words stuck in his throat, as he saw that they would only laugh at his warning. So he adopted the air of a doomed and isolated witness to tragic omens. This mood was sharply interrupted by the young lieutenant, who began to beat him with the flat of his sword and accuse him of lagging behind.

The brigade halted after a time, and the "religious" **metaphor** once more occupies the youth's mind. The gloom of the forest is a "cathedral light"; the "floating smoke" (from the rifles) goes up in white, compact balls. A number of the men began to build little protective mounds. They even argued about the merits of small ones over large ones, and over the correct postures to be assumed during combat. (The veterans, meanwhile, were "digging at the ground like terriers.") In a short time they were ordered to move on. The youth's loud complaints at this lack of consideration were met by the tall soldier's calm explanation. Soon, in another place, they had erected another line of entrenchments, ate their noon meal behind still another, and were moved from that in turn. They seemed to be wandering about aimlessly. The youth had been taught that man became "another thing" in battle, and in this change he saw his salvation. His impatience inevitably led him back to his theory that this was all a "blue demonstration." He wished either to return to camp or to go into battle and discover that he was indeed "a man of traditional courage." The tall soldier chewed philosophically on a sandwich of cracker and pork, while the loud soldier grunted sarcastically and the youth continued to fidget. The loud soldier declared his desire to get into a fight, while the tall soldier, "red-faced, swallowed another sandwich as if taking poison in despair." But as he chewed he became quiet, lost in blissful contemplation of the food he had swallowed. "His spirit seemed to be communing with the viands." His equanimity appeared to be a result of his eating at every opportunity. He had not even raised his voice when he had been ordered to leave behind the little entrenchments he had made, "each of which had been an engineering feat worthy of being made sacred to the name of his grandmother."

Comment

Any interpretation of the tall soldier's meaning to the story (especially the significance of the manner of his death at the end of Chapter 9) must face up to these earlier suggestions of his status as a "communicant" in some unspecified religion. (Crane later refers to him, in fact, as a "devotee of some mad religion.") A widely held opinion (which originated with R. W. Stallman) is that Jim Conklin is a symbol of Jesus Christ, and that his death is a sacrificial death through which Henry Fleming achieves his redemption. But here we note clearly that the tall soldier is defined as a "communicant," not as a sacrificial object.

The regiment moved out in the afternoon and the youth continued to grapple with his problem. Even death appeared to him as a welcome conclusion. It was, after all, nothing but rest, and he was surprised that he had made such a stir about it. Meanwhile the skirmishing went on, and he heard cheering mingled with the sound of distant firing. Then the skirmishers appeared on the run, rifle flashes were to be seen, clouds of smoke rolled "insolently" across the field, and the battle din increased to a tremendous roar. The youth was spellbound, his eyes wide and busy, and his mouth hanging open. In his astonishment he felt a "heavy and sad hand" on his shoulder. It was the loud soldier. Pale, his lips trembling, he handed the youth a packet enclosed in a yellow envelope. The youth started in surprise, but the other "gave him a glance as from the depths of a tomb, and raised his limp hand in a prophetic manner and turned away."

Comment

It should be noted that the religious **metaphor** is not confined (among the human figures) to Jim Conklin. It is here used of Wilson, who is momentarily regarded as a "prophet," crying "from the depths" (perhaps a hint of Psalm 129 - De profundis clamavi, "Out of the depths I have cried unto thee, O Lord!", or possibly of the story of Lazarus, speaking from the tomb).

SUMMARY

1. Action: The regiment has marched for another day, and crosses the river at nightfall. After some days they are plunged into battle, where the youth confronts its ugliness and chaos. The youth continues to ponder; Conklin maintains a philosophical calm; and Wilson is overcome by maudlin and gloomy thoughts of death.

2. The regiment comes further under the influence of nature (the clothes - shedding **episode**) and thus of instinctual response, but they remain "fresh fish" in the eyes of the veterans (as the similarity of headgear suggests).

3. The tension between instinct and calculation is pointed up in the sudden starts and pauses in the chapter, wherein the youth is sometimes forced to act on impulse, and must make greater efforts to find leisure for reflection. The same antithesis is indicated in the contrast between the recruits who argue about proper postures, and the veterans who dig like terriers.

4. Continued image patterns:

    a. The classical-heroic **theme** - here seen mainly in the **allusion** to the myth of Cadmus, but also in such casual epithets as that of the "wine-tinted water."

    b. The religious **metaphor** - references to the "blood-swollen god of war," the "cathedral light of the forest," to Wilson as a "prophet," and especially to Conklin as a "communicant" in "blissful contemplation."

5. Stylistic effects:

    a. Verbal **irony** - such phrases as "busy as bees," and "projected piteously."

    b. Personification - for example, "the smoke clouds went slowly and insolently."

    c. Elevated style - Conklin's trenches, for instance, being called "engineering feats worthy of being made sacred," etc.

6. Characterization: By far the most important detail in the chapter is the youth's sudden aspiration to see a glorious scene of battle and his consequent disappointment at the actual confusion which greeted him, together with the psychological depression which followed.

CHAPTER 4

The brigade halted at the edge of a grove, and the new recruits passed rumors about eagerly. There is some agitated gossip about various officers (Perry, Carrott, Hannis, and Hasbrouck), a rumor that the general promised to take command of the 304th himself, and a report of a boast made by one of the 140th Maine regiment about the "five thousand" of the enemy they had just killed. (The Maine soldier is referred to as Bill, and he turns out to be the man whose foot was trod on during the march.) Bill is reported as having been willing to give up his hand for his country, but reluctant to have "every dumb bushwhacker in th' kentry walkin' 'round on it." He went to the hospital, regardless of the fight; the doctor wanted to amputate three fingers, but "he raised a heluva row," the reporting soldier continued, "he's a funny feller."

> **Comment**

The concepts of courage, mere heroics, and cowardice are here presented in an uneasy poise. Bill is alleged not to be "easily scared," yet his willingness to give "his hand to his country" jibes oddly with such genuinely heroic offers as Nathan Hale's to "give his life for his country." And his willingness to go to the hospital as well as the row over having the fingers amputated (which appears to have been an instant cure for malingering) suggest that he is far from a model of bravery. Furthermore, the reference to amputation anticipates the youth's later thought (Chapter 5) that he might save himself from annihilation by "amputating" himself from the regiment, while the noncommittal description of Bill as "a funny feller" looks forward to such appraisals as that the tattered man makes of the tall soldier in death: "Well, he was a reg'lar jim-dandy .... It was a funny thing." This is a minor manifestation of the **theme** that war does extraordinary things to the emotions - brings about a severe psychological wrenching.

As the men crouched there, the din of battle swelled, shells screamed overhead, and bullets whistled through the trees. The lieutenant of the company was shot in the hand, and he swore so magnificently that a nervous laugh broke out along the line - his profanity relieved the tensions of the moment. "He held the wounded member carefully away from his side so that the blood would not drip upon his trousers."

> **Comment**

The word "member," here used of the hand - in fact, the very idea of the relationship of members to an organic whole - looks ahead to the youth's embodiment of his problem of courage in the image of the relationship of members and whole, individual part and total unit, and is related also to the amputation motif just alluded to.

While the captain and the lieutenant dispute about how to bind the wound, the battle flag is seen in the distance being "jerked about madly," seeming to try "to free itself from an agony." Men emerge from the smoke fleeing, and the flag sinks down, as if in a "gesture of despair." As the soldiers of the 304th retreat (the youth is at the rear, with the reserves) they hear jeers and catcalls from the veterans on the flanks. The youth saw officers, cursing like highwaymen, striking about in an effort to stem the rout. One raged like a spoiled child. Another looked as if he had been roused from bed to go to a fire. Oaths and grim jokes went unheeded by the "mad current" of soldiery on its way to the rear. The youth thought that he must certainly flee, if only he could get control of his legs. The stampede seemed to be a flood that could drag sticks, stones and men from the ground. The "monster" that caused the flight did not immediately appear, or (so the youth thought) he would very likely take to his heels.

SUMMARY

This short chapter occupies a very short period of time - only a few minutes before an encounter, and a few (perhaps only seconds) during it. It has the following specific functions:

1. It brings the youth a step nearer to actual combat, and allows him enough leisure to decide that flight from battle is a distinct possibility for him.

2. It provides serious and comic (the "Bill" **episode**) versions of courageous actions.

3. It introduces the terminology of "amputation" and "members," which will be elaborated upon in later chapters.

4. It presents a concrete picture of the literal and the emotional turbulence of battle, in the nightmarish picture of cursing officers, jeering veterans, and terrified recruits.

CHAPTER 5

The fifth chapter opens in the lull before the counterattack by the soldiers in gray. Phantasms from his early boyhood thronged in upon the youth's mind - the circus parade, with a dingy lady on a white horse, a band in a faded chariot, and an old fellow on a cracker box in front of a store, a "thousand details of color and form." The cry arose, "Here they come," and there was a feverish flurry to have cartridges at hand and guns ready. Suddenly they came running, a "brown swarm" of yelling men swinging rifles and following a flag which was tilted forward. The youth began to wonder if his gun was actually loaded, when his thoughts were interrupted by the vision of a hatless general exhorting the colonel of the 304th to hold them back, and the colonel stammering in reply that they would do their best. The general rode off, making a "passionate gesture," the colonel scolded like a "wet parrot," and the captain of the youth's company "coaxed in schoolmistress fashion." The youth was perspiring freely, his mouth hanging open. One glance at the foe and he forgot to wonder about his gun's being loaded, but began to fire it as if it were an automatic affair. "He suddenly lost concern for himself, and forgot to look at a menacing fate. He became not a man but a member ... He was welded into a common personality which was dominated by a single desire. For some moments he could not flee, no more than a little finger can commit a revolution from a hand."

| Comment

It is significant that the youth's temporary "courage" at this point (he will of course flee before long) is a result of a feeling of membership in a common personality. But the feeling is still too much the result of reflection, and too much dependent on the closeness and solidity of the other members.

The noise gives him assurance; his sense of the regiment as a firework proceeding "superior to circumstance," the consciousness of his comrades' presence, and his sense of a "subtle battle brotherhood" seem necessary to sustain his nerve. Furthermore, it is a courage as yet untried by any real challenges. These are soon to begin, as his blistering sweat, cracking eyeballs, and roaring ears are followed by a red rage. His one-shot rifle gives him a feeling of impotency against the "swirling battle phantoms." He had to fight for air, as a babe who is being smothered fights the deadly blankets.

| Comment

The comparison with the smothering baby is far from casual. (Shortly after, in fact, the man at his elbow is described as "babbling ... soft and tender like the monologue of a babe.") Battle reduces the youth to a condition of psychological infancy, necessitating the "education" which his later experiences provide.

In addition to the babbling man, there are sounds of snarling, imprecation, and prayer, forming a chantlike undercurrent to the war march (that is, the sounds of rifles and cannon). The tall soldier swore "curious oaths," and another man plaintively wondered aloud why they had not been given support.

THE RED BADGE OF COURAGE

The youth listened to all this through the haze of a "battle sleep." None of the heroic poses which he had earlier envisioned were at all in evidence. Men were "surging" in impossible attitudes, cartridge-box flaps "bobbed idiotically," and rifles were jerked and fired aimlessly at forms which had been increasing in size "like puppets under a magician's hand" (even the "war as drama" **metaphor** here degenerates into a puppet show). The officers, too, appear ridiculous, looking like awkward and boisterous children as they bob to and fro, give vent to extraordinary howls, and practically stand on their heads in excitement. The lieutenant had to pummel a deserting soldier back into line and even help him to load his gun. The captain had been killed earlier, and his face bore an "astonished and sorrowful look"; the babbling man, his head grazed by a bullet, was bleeding freely; another man, shot in the stomach, sat down with a rueful gaze.

At last the attack was turned back. The enemy departed, leaving their debris behind. Some of the youth's regiment whooped in a frenzy; others remained silent. The youth became aware of the suffocating atmosphere and took a long drink of the warm water in his canteen. Along the line went the triumphant claim, "We've helt 'em back; derned if we haven't." And the narrator remarks, "The men said it blissfully, leering at each other with dirty smiles."

| Comment

A leer is (according to a common dictionary definition) "a sly look or sidewise glance expressing salacious desire, malicious intent, knowing complicity, etc." While "dirty smiles" may refer merely to the grime on the men's faces, there is a certain ambiguity about the entire sentence; it may well be meant by

BRIGHT NOTES STUDY GUIDE

Crane to suggest (what is a psychological commonplace) that there is a subtle sexual aspect to the martial drive, just as there is to the enthusiastic frenzies of certain primitive religious rites (both of which ideas enter into the pattern of **imagery** in the closing chapters of the book).

At last finding leisure to look about, the youth noticed ghastly bodies lying in grotesquely twisted attitudes. From the rear of the grove came a volley of shells from a number of guns which "squatted in a row like savage chiefs" as if they were holding a "grim pow-wow." Processions of wounded men, masses of troops, sounds of cheering and combat, the noise of guns, all gradually relinquish their hold on the youth's attention, and he suddenly notices with a thrill the striped emblem of his country, looking "like a beautiful bird undaunted in a storm." His gaze turns upward, and he notices in astonishment the blue, pure sky and the gleaming sun. "It was surprising that Nature had gone tranquilly on with her golden process in the midst of so much devilment."

SUMMARY

This chapter covers the first attack to which the youth is directly exposed. He is among the reserves of the 304th, who stand firm and repulse the enemy. It is mainly concerned with the youth's physiological responses to combat, and the psychological changes they bring. Specifically:

1. As before, characters are put before us in brief, epitomizing phrases: a hatless general who makes a "passionate gesture" and gallops away; a stammering, petulant colonel: the captain who coaxes his troops like a schoolmistress, and tells them to hold their fire

until they are close up (ironically, he is among the first to be killed); the valiant lieutenant.

2. The question of the youth's "courage" is related to his sense of "membership" in a common personality, and is thus tied in with earlier images of bodily "members" and "amputation."

3. Imagery:

   a. The "religious" **metaphor** is not prominent except for an **allusion** to the imprecations of the men as a "chantlike" undercurrent to the war march.

   b. The "infancy" figure appears in the **simile** which compares the youth to a choking baby, as well as in the childlike actions of the officers, and the babbling man.

   c. The "war as drama" figure is seen in the "puppet" **metaphor**, and in the lieutenant's "acting a little isolated scene" with a deserter.

4. Perhaps the finest contribution this chapter makes is to present the ghastly, phantasmagoric pattern of sound (cannon din, curious oaths, infantile monologue), form (idiotic jerks, bobbings, and contortions), and color (black figures of gunners, dominating red of the flag, pure blue sky) which assails the youth's senses.

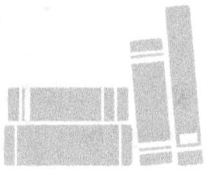

THE RED BADGE OF COURAGE

TEXTUAL ANALYSIS

CHAPTERS 6-11

CHAPTER 6

This chapter opens with the youth in a mood of elation - a premature "ecstasy of self-satisfaction." He saw himself as a magnificent warrior, a fine fellow, who had achieved ideals which he had formerly considered beyond him. Amid a general atmosphere of sociability, of handshakings and earnest conversations, the youth luxuriated. In amazed consternation they were suddenly forced to hero the cry of "Here they come ag'in," and to look toward the wood to see the tilted flag speeding forward once more. Once more, too, the bursting shells and the din. They groaned, fretted, and complained. A voice expressed the wish that its hand had been trodden on by Bill Smithers, instead of the reverse, after which the narrator remarks that the "sore joints of the regiment creaked as it ... floundered into position." The youth half expected the enemy to apologize and retire gracefully. But the firing began, and the sheets of flame and clouds of smoke arose again. Crane describes the youth at this point in one of his most objective bits of description: "Into the youth's eyes there came a look that one can see in the orbs of a jaded horse. His neck was quivering with nervous weakness and the muscles of his arms felt numb and bloodless. His hands, too, seemed large and awkward as if he was wearing invisible mittens. And there was a great uncertainty about his knee joints."

His comrades' earlier complaints came back to him, and he began to exaggerate the skill and bravery of the enemy, who, he thought, must be machines, "wound up perhaps to fight until sundown." He was reeling from exhaustion, but he fired at an approaching cluster, then stopped. He caught glimpses of men running like pursued imps, and the whole scene became for him "an onslaught of redoubtable dragons. He became like the man who lost his legs at the approach of the red and green monster" (apparently an **allusion** to some folklore or fairy-tale motif). A man who had been firing by his side, suddenly stopped and fled, while another lad, who a moment before had been a paragon of courage, broke and ran. The youth seemed to receive a sudden illumination - a revelation. "He, too, threw down his gun and fled. There was no shame in his face. He ran like a rabbit." Others also scampered away from the fight, and Henry, yelling in fright, swung about and ran.

Comment

Crane is at considerable pains to point out the reflexive, compulsive nature of the youth's act. He has been taken by surprise; he is exhausted; his imagination is at its most susceptible. Indeed, all his former speculations about losing control of his legs, as well as the multiplicity of images depicting the enemy as a serpent or dragon of some sort, blend in his vision of himself as the man who lost his legs at the monster's approach. Furthermore, the "mystic brotherhood" or organic member-ship of his regiment is shattered not by the youth, but by the feverish rifleman and the courageous lad nearby, both of whom turn tail and run.

In his panic the youth takes "great leaps" toward the rear, abandoning rifle and cap on the way. Running like a blind man, he first avoids the sword of the bawling lieutenant, then later falls heavily against a tree. As he ran his fears magnified, and he thought the battle noises were stones about to crush him. Striving not to be one of the dragon's initial mouthfuls, he sprinted insanely to the rear. Crossing a field he found himself amidst exploding shells, so that he was forced to go twisting off through some bushes. The sight of a battery firing methodically and coolly aroused in him only a sort of scornful pity, as did the face of a youthful rider, and even the very guns themselves - "six good comrades, in a bold row." He found it hard to understand the reason why a brigade should be going to the help of its fellows, hastening forward to be swallowed up by the war god. Either they were some wondrous breed of men, or else they were outright fools. As he went on the youth slackened his pace, since he had left "the place of noises."

After a time he came upon a general seated on horseback - a quiet man, who looked like a businessman in a fluctuating market. The youth even imagined that the general might call upon him for advice. He felt like thrashing him for standing so calmly in one spot, and making no effort to save life by ordering a retreat. Skulking about, he overheard the general issuing orders, through a messenger on a fine chestnut horse, for a regiment to be detached to back up the center. Shortly thereafter the general bounced excitedly in his saddle, joyous with the realization that the line had held. After sending word to follow up this success, he "beamed upon the earth like a sun," and "held a little carnival of joy on horseback."

Comment

Crane's ironic reflections on the youth for his failure to comprehend the necessity of professional calm on the part of the general suddenly turn against the general himself, as we perceive that his speech patterns, his instant enthusiasm, and his almost boyish glee at his success are not vastly different from that of the men themselves at their earlier success.

SUMMARY

Chapter 6 treats of the temporary respite enjoyed by the reserves of the 304th, the second charge by the gray line, the boy's flight, and his reactions as he flees to two encounters: the "precise gunners" of a battery; and a quiet general on horseback. His first reaction is one of pity and scorn, but by the end of the chapter there is a slight shaking of his smugness.

1. This crucial chapter provides the reader with an insight into the psychology of flight. The youth is surprised and exhausted (he is compared to a jaded horse). Two staunch comrades at his side flee unabashedly - one runs "like a rabbit," others "scamper away through the smoke," and the youth himself is compared to the "proverbial chicken" (presumably, the "chicken with his head chopped off," who runs about wildly on surviving nervous impulses). Furthermore, it appears to him that the "regiment is leaving him behind," rather than the reverse.

2. A number of thematic images reappear in forms which anticipate the youth's desertion:

   a. The "god of war" - "the slaves toiling in the temple of this god began to feel rebellion at his harsh tasks."

   b. The regiment as "body" - "the sore joints of the regiment creaked as it painfully floundered into position to repulse."

   c. The enemy as "serpent" - the youth "became like the man who lost his legs at the approach of the red and green monster."

   d. The "automation" figure - it is now the enemy which the youth imagines to be "machines of steel ... wound up to fight until sundown."

CHAPTER 7

With mingled feelings of shame, amazement, and anger, the youth listened to the cheers which told of a blue success. He tried to tell himself that he had done right in rescuing himself - one little piece which could later rejoin its fellows. His action, he felt, had been correct, commendable, wise. As he thought of his comrades who had remained, his feelings turned to bitterness at their stupidity - a stupidity which had betrayed him. His own enlightened farsightedness had been betrayed by fools. Angry rationalization suddenly passed into apprehension, as he wondered what howls of derision would greet him when he returned to camp, then into acute pity, and finally into a "dull, animal-like rebellion against his fellows." With head bowed, brain in an agonized confusion, and guilt-ridden eyes, he shambled along.

Leaving the open fields, he entered a thick wood, trying to escape the sounds of the rifles. Vines and bushes were spread out like bouquets. Sprays and saplings "cried out" as he trampled among them. "He could not conciliate the forest," and, afraid lest the sounds should bring men to see him "he went far, seeking dark and intricate places."

Comment

The "intricate" places may be compared to the "intricate" hole which served as a door to his hut in Chapter 1, both suggestive of penetration into the dimmer regions of the psyche.

The sounds of war grow faint in the distance, and the sun, "suddenly apparent, blazed among the trees," while insects made rhythmical noises in unison. Nature now appears to him in a most idealized form. The landscape is a "fair field holding life"; Nature is a "woman with a deep aversion to tragedy." Throwing a pine cone at a squirrel, he watched it run in fear, and was convinced that this was the law. Danger means flight. The youth "wended, feeling that Nature was of his mind."

Comment

The picture the youth entertains is of course false, and will be shattered by the shocking confrontation with the corpse which quickly ensues. The scene as he now views it is the typical "ideal landscape" of so many medieval poems, in which green banks, singing birds, and burgeoning trees are presided over by the goddess Natura. The "fair field holding life" is like fourteenth-century writer William Langland's "faire fielde ful of folke" at the opening of his *Piers Ploughman*; the medieval pageantry of the scene is underlined by the archaic **connotations** of the verb "wended."

There is a glancing reference to another, less favorable, aspect of nature in the swamp, bog tufts, and oily mire which he has to pass through, but at length he reached an enclosure, a "chapel" formed by arching boughs, carpeted with pine needles, an illuminated in a "religious half light." Horror - stricken, he observed a corpse with its back against a tree. The blue uniform had faded to a melancholy green (perhaps it is being reassumed into nature). The eyes were fishlike, the mouth an appalling yellow, and ants crawled along the face. The youth shrieked and stood immobile for several moments exchanging glances with the thing, then cautiously retreated, while his feet caught in brambles and his mind subtly offered the perverse suggestion that he go back and touch the corpse. Finally, he fled.

Comment

The "religious **metaphor**" and the nature **imagery** come into shocking collision in this scene. The youth, thinking he is escaping from the "swollen war god" into an idyllic earthly paradise (and unconscious of the painful reminders in the blazing sun and the oily mire) stumbles into the very heart of nature and discovers there that She is in effect the divinity to whom war makes its sacrifices. Ironically, even the sacrifice lacks the clean barbarism of knife and bleeding victim, and is instead merely the deposit of a putrescent mass.

SUMMARY

This short chapter contains one of the two or three most shocking **episodes** which contribute to the maturing of the youth's emotional and intellectual attitudes toward war and courage. He begins by congratulating himself on his sagacious intellect, and escapes from the nagging sense of guilt by burying himself in the bosom of Nature, where he

> at first finds confirmation of the rightness of his actions, but soon undergoes a horrifying shaking of his purpose, when he encounters the decaying body of the soldier.

CHAPTER 8

The sardonic voice of the narrator opens this chapter by continued references to the hymns chanted by the trees. Suddenly, a "crimson roar" was heard in the distance. His mind was again in a turmoil, and he began to run toward the battle, telling himself that one ought to be a spectator at such a tremendous clash. The ear-shaking thunder of the battle caused him to reflect that the fight he had been involved in was nothing but "perfunctory popping." He began to take his own and his mates' initial attitude of seriousness toward the battle with a sort of wry humor. They had supposed that their deeds of glory would cut their names "deep into everlasting tablets of brass," and that their reputations would be forever enshrined "in the hearts of their countrymen." But he reflected that perhaps even such illusions might be good, if they prevented wholesale flight from battle.

Comment

This echo of Henry Lee's eulogy on George Washington - "first in war, first in peace, and first in the hearts of his countrymen" - epitomizes the publicly accepted standard of heroism. As he thus formulates it, the youth appears to be thinking ironically, but his **irony** is neither total nor absolute, and he begins to see good in gestures of heroism.

As the youth hastened on, the brambles and trees formed chains which held him back and he reflected with a "fine bitterness" on the new resistance of the forest (to letting him pass into battle) considering its previous hostility (its interference as he had run away, and the horror of the "chapel" scene). Obstinately he pressed on, fascinated by the image of battle as "the grinding of an immense and terrible machine," producing corpses. He passed through a field littered with clothes and guns, a newspaper, and a group of corpses "keeping mournful company." He felt like an invader in the place, and hurried on. Finally, the youth arrived at a road, along which came a "blood - stained crowd" of men, whose curses and groans mingled with the cheers of others and the "courageous words of the artillery and the spiteful sentences of the musketry." Against the stupendous din and pageantry of the battle, this "steady current of the maimed" appeared like a parade of contorted puppets. A man with a shoeful of blood hopped like a schoolboy in a game; another appeared to be imitating "some sublime drum major." Still another had the gray seal of death on his face (this is Jim Conklin, though the youth doesn't recognize him); his hands were bloody, he stalked like a specter, staring into the unknown.

A wounded officer peevishly criticized his bearers and bellowed at those blocking his way. In reply, they told him to be damned. The shoulder of one of the bearers knocked against the spectral soldier (Conklin). At this point the youth fell in with the melancholy march.

A tattered man, stained with blood and powder, trudged along "listening with eagerness and much humility to the lurid descriptions of a bearded sergeant. His lean features wore an expression of awe and admiration. He was like a listener in a country store to wondrous tales told among the sugar barrels ... His mouth was agape in yokel fashion."

> **Comment**

This description well illustrates the problem of deciding whether the narrator is reporting his own interpretation of events, or the youth's. On the one hand we are given a number of idealizing details: the formulaic description "the tattered man"; his "humility" and "lean features"; his comparison to a "listener ... to wondrous tales." On the other hand, we note the reference to the country store and the sugar barrels, the entire description terminating in the sharply contrasted sentences, "He eyed the story-teller with unspeakable wonder," and "His mouth was agape in yokel fashion." It is probably best to consider this kind of antithesis as a reflection of the tension in the youth's own conflicting attitudes. He vacillates between a vision of heroic warriors, whose deeds and postures are charged with a kind of sanctified significance, and a vision of aimlessly cavorting puppets.

The youth noted that the tattered soldier had a gentle voice, pleading eyes, and wounds in his head and arm. In an apologetic manner, he tried to engage Fleming in conversation about the battle. He had much praise for the way the boys had fought, and after recounting a dialogue in which a Georgia soldier had told him across a picket line that the blue soldiers would run at the sound of a gun, he ended, "No, sir! They fit, an' fit, an' fit." For a while his homely face "was suffused with a light of love" for the army; then, suddenly, he turned to the youth and inquired where he was hit. In a panic Fleming turned and slid away, forehead flushed and fingers nervously picking at a button.

SUMMARY

> This brief chapter advances the plot in a few specific ways:
>
> 1. The youth's certainty that he was right in fleeing is seen to be modified.
>
> 2. He meets the "spectral soldier" - Conklin, though he doesn't recognize him - and this underscores the terrible metamorphosis which war brings about in persons.
>
> 3. His encounter with the tattered soldier is the beginning of his suffering of the shame of his flight.

CHAPTER 9

The youth fell back in the procession of the wounded, out of sight of the tattered soldier. Amidst the bleeding throng he felt that his shame was on display, and he glanced about furtively. He was envious of them; he wished that he, too, had "a wound, a red badge of courage."

Comment

This is the first time that the phrase "red badge of courage" had appeared in the book.

The spectral soldier stalked at his side, his gray face causing others to gather about and slow their pace to his. With lips tightly closed, he signed them to go on; he seemed to be "taking infinite care not to arouse the passion of his wounds." Suddenly the youth recognized his waxlike features and screamed in horror, "Gawd! Jim Conklin!" Jim made a commonplace gesture and held out his gory hand. As the youth lamented over him in an inarticulate way, Conklin made gestures of concern about the youth's own adventures in the day's fighting. He seemed bewildered about his own wound, and as Henry put forth arms to assist him, he appeared to be overcome by terror and his face turned to "a semblance of gray paste." In a shaky whisper he confided to Henry his fear of being run over by the artillery wagons, and the youth promised to take care of him, though the gulpings in his throat made him speak somewhat inaccurately. The tall soldier clung "babelike" to the youth's arm, and began to whine for assistance. Sobbing in anguish, Henry could only make fantastic gestures to express his loyalty. All of a sudden, the tall soldier recovered himself and went forward with "mysterious purpose." At the suggestion of the tattered soldier Henry tried to grasp Jim's arm and lead him off the road, out of the way of an approaching artillery battery. Wrenching free, Conklin dashed off through the field toward a clump of bushes, with the youth and the tattered soldier in pursuit. As they overtook him, the tall soldier pleaded to be left alone and lurched ahead with "ritelike" movements. He resembled "a devotee of a mad religion," and they stood off in awe of him. Finally he became motionless, and with figure erect and bloody hands at his side he waited for the thing he had come to meet. "He was at the rendezvous."

Comment

It has been suggested that Alan Seeger's fine poem of World War I, "I have a rendezvous with Death," owes its title (and perhaps its basic conception) to this passage of Crane's. The poem concludes:

... I've a rendezvous with Death At midnight in some flaming town, When Spring trips north again this year, And I to my pledged word am true, I shall not fail that rendezvous.

After a brief silence, Conklin's chest began to heave, with increasing violence "as if an animal was within and was kicking and tumbling furiously to be free."

Comment

Crane's technique of inversion (such as the imputation of will and purpose to nature at the same time that he practically denies it to human beings) reaches its extreme form in this image, in which the traditional figure of the spiritual soul striving for release from the animal body becomes an animal struggling to be free of a cage or trap. Even the non - Christian twentieth - century Irish poet W. B. Yeats (in "Sailing to Byzantium") speaks of his heart as "sick with desire / And fastened to a dying animal."

The youth writhed at the sight and fell to the ground, wailing. Conklin's form suddenly stiffened; a "creeping strangeness" came over him and he danced a sort of "hideous hornpipe," with his arms flailing about in "imp-like enthusiasm." He fell forward like a tree, and his left shoulder struck the ground after which the body "seemed to bounce a little way from the earth." The face was pastelike, the mouth open and the teeth showing in a laugh. His side looked as though it had been chewed by wolves. The youth shook his fist at the battlefield, and (the famous ending) "the red sun was pasted in the sky like a wafer."

Comment

This line has provoked a good deal of discussion and controversy, mainly centering on the question of whether the word "wafer" is to be taken merely as "sealing wafer" (the wax seal for an envelope) or "communion wafer" (the sacramental form of Christ's body), and, consequently, whether the image should be regarded simply as a bit of naturalistic description or as a symbolic **allusion** to the death of Conklin as a Christ - figure through whose "sacrifice" Henry Fleming achieves his "redemption." In support of the symbolic interpretation, notice should of course be taken of the continuing religious **metaphor** appearing in all the earlier chapters, as well as the references to Conklin's bloody hands, his wounded side, and the "passion of his wounds." Somewhat less impressive details for purposes of argument are his initials (J. C., for Jesus Christ?) and the description of his body as seeming "to bounce a little way from the earth" (the Resurrection?). Against the symbolic reading - at least in its form of a consistent and absolute analogy between Christ and Conklin - are any number of other details, such as his identification as a "devotee of a mad religion" (which hardly squares with the relationship of Christ to Christianity). [See "Critical Commentary" for fuller treatment of this point.]

CHAPTER 10

This chapter opens with a sharp contrast of attitudes toward Conklin's death. The tattered man muses thoughtfully, and can only remark, "Well, he was a reg'lar jim-dandy," while the youth throws himself on the ground in an agony of grief. But looking up suddenly he observed that the tattered soldier was himself swaying uncertainly on his legs and had grown pale. To Henry's apprehensive words, however, he replied merely that all he needed was some pea soup and a good bed. As they gazed together at the corpse, the youth "murmured something," and his companion simply repeated his earlier comment, "Well, he was a jim-dandy, wa'nt'e?"

| Comment

The youth's "murmur" is either one of Crane's not infrequent exasperatingly vague declarations, or else is meant to suggest, perhaps, that his response to Conklin's "ritual" death is an automatic, nonverbal murmur akin to the "chanted chorus" of insects and birds in the cathedral of the forest - another sign of his gradual assimilation into the pattern of nature.

As they stole away from the fallen body, the tattered soldier groaned once more, and the youth wondered if he was to be the "tortured witness" of another death. But his friend reassured him with lighthearted words that he was not about to die.

The tattered soldier then thinks of his own wound and how he received it. He was fighting when all of a sudden a fellow alongside (Tom Jamison) began to swear at him for not noticing that he had been shot. He had put his hand up to his head and discovered a wound, "hollered" and ran, and then felt another hit in the arm. He would be fighting yet, he mused, if it hadn't been for Tom Jamison. (Another instance of the part played by chance in the matter of courage.) Quickly, the tattered man leaves the subject of his own wounds, and turns to the youth, asking him where his wound is "located." It might be inside, he goes on, "an' them plays thunder." It might be some "queer kind 'a hurt," he decides, and asks again where it is "located."

| Comment

The tattered man's insistence here, particularly his desire to know where Henry's wound in "located" (as if it were some precise point, to be graphed with coordinates) underscores the youth's own problem of finding the locus of courage (in heart? head? legs and arms?).

In rage and exasperation, the youth dismisses the tattered man's questions. His companion's curiosity was always "upraising the ghost of shame." With a glance of hatred and contempt he said good-bye to the other, who thereupon floundered in a spate of half-formed statements and questions, finally giving in to hallucinations in which he saw the youth as Tom Jamison, and chided him for going away while his wound needed caring for. As the youth climbed a fence he looked back to see the tattered man wandering about helplessly in a field. The narrator declares that the youth "thought that he wished he was dead" and "believed that he envied" the dead men whose bodies lay strewn over the battlefield. The tattered man's questions were a sign of a pitilessly probing society, sure to reveal the crime in his bosom. He could not "defend himself against this agency."

Comment

The youth's identification of his own fraternity - his fellow soldiers - as an "enemy" against which he must "defend" himself breaks down even further the easy categories of "friend" and "enemy" and thus contributes to his growing sense that "courage," whatever it might be, is not to be achieved through any sort of analytical formula.

SUMMARY

This chapter clearly belongs to the "tattered man," and raises important questions about his significance for the total meaning of the book. The following are some of the contributions this chapter makes:

1. Aside from its conformity to Crane's general method of identification through an epitomizing phrase ("tall soldier," etc.) the description "tattered man" provokes certain ambiguous responses in the reader. Like a baggy-pants clown, he combines humor and pathos, in a vague gamut of echoes between such extremes as the nursery-rhyme "man all tattered and torn" and the motley-garbed fool in King Lear.

2. Not only is the "tattered man" an objectively ambiguous figure, but his own responses to the horror of wounds and death ("fun," "funny," "queer," "the funniest thing," "a reg'lar jim-dandy," etc.) symbolize the bizarre warping of emotions that the nightmare of battle can produce. Even the friend, Tom Jamison, who sympathetically calls attention to this wound does so with a bellowed curse - "yeh blamed infernal."

3. In realistic terms the "tattered soldier's persistent questioning leads the youth to the realization that he can not possibly hope to keep his crime concealed; in metaphoric terms the ambiguity which radiates from the "tattered soldier's" action is matched by the youth's imaginative embodiment of his own army as an "enemy" against which he must defend himself.

CHAPTER 11

Henry becomes aware of the increasing "furnace roar" of the battle; brown clouds floated to the heights, the noise approached, and the woods "filtered men."

Comment

The naturalistic (and traditional) description of battle noise as a roar is significantly qualified here. "Furnace roar" and "filtering" woods suggest that battle is a kind of chemical process in which things are purified by fire, an image which looks back to Chapter 2 in which the youth had compared his own desire for blaze, blood, and danger, to the chemist's requirements for ingredients to be employed in an analytical process.

The roadway was a confused jumble of retreating men, wagons, and horses. It was comforting to the youth, who was able to use the uproar to magnify in his mind the horrors of the battle, and thus to vindicate his own desertion. Presently an advancing column of infantry appeared, like a sinuous serpent, pushing forward by main force and swearing "many strange oaths." They were eager to confront the enemy, proud of their forward rush, filled with a "fine feeling" of importance. They were a reproach to the youth, just as the retreating hordes were a vindication. He wondered what they could have eaten, that they could be in such a hurry to meet their doom. They inspired in him once more romantic visions of himself as a dashing figure "leading lurid charges" and standing calmly in the face of danger. Uplifted by these thoughts he felt a quiver of war desire, knew the frenzy of a successful charge. "For a few moments he was sublime." Then, as he reflected on the difficulties of the thing, he hesitated. Each doubt, for a time, was easily resolved. He had no rifle - yet rifles abounded on the field. He could not find his regiment - yet he could fight with any regiment. He might be observed skulking back by some of his comrades - yet in the fight his face would be hidden. Finally, however, his "courage expended itself on these objection." And in any case various physical ailments had begun to cry out. He had a scorching thirst; his skin was dry; his bones ached; his feet were sore. Hunger was causing him to sway; it blurred his sight. It was impossible, he now thought, that he should ever be a hero. "He was a craven loon." Yet a certain "mothlike quality" within him kept him near the battle.

Comment

This is a reference of course to the fable of the moth and the flame (instinctively it seeks the flame and is consumed by it). In this image the human-as-animal figure and the battle-as-fire figure merge. It is a reminder that instinct continually operates in the youth to offset the decisions arrived at speculatively.

    The youth wished to discover who was winning, and had to admit (apologetically) to his conscience that a defeat would be a favorable thing for him; in the general rout he could easily convince others that he had not run faster or farther than they. He began to construct an elaborate justification for his welcoming to defeat. Other defeats had been mourned for a while but were in time forgotten. And after all it was the generals, not the men, who had to bear the brunt to public criticism. Indeed, public opinion would probably hit upon the wrong general anyway, and he would then be forced to spend his remaining days composing replies to the allegations of his failure - unfortunate, but hardly of any consequence to Henry Fleming. He himself would be vindicated. A prophet who predicts a flood should be the first man to climb a tree. Moral vindication seemed very necessary to him. Unaccountably, these self-glorifying thoughts gave way to self - denunciation. He saw himself now as a villain, and imagined his comrades' dripping corpses tacitly rebuking him as their murderer. Once more he envied the corpses. Many of them no doubt would receive their laurels from tradition without having really been tested. Theirs would be stolen crowns and robes of sham.

But defeat of the blue army quickly appeared to him as unthinkable. The mighty blue machine would turn out victories "as a contrivance turns out buttons." He tried to think of a "fine tale" with which he could turn back the jeers which we certain to come his way, but he found that it was impossible. They were all vulnerable. He would be able to meet sneers and laughter only with stammering hesitation. He would become an object of insolence and scorn - a "slang phrase."

SUMMARY

This chapter is notable for its pattern of quick alternation between optimism and despair, self-scorn and self-glorification, romantic visions and realistic descriptions. In this respect, it conveys well the turmoil of the mind lost in the agony of rationalization continually punctured by true perceptions. In addition:

1. The figure of battle as furnace (roaring and flaming), which in any case carries almost mythic **connotations** of "purification by fire," catches up earlier suggestions of the "chemistry of battle" and looks ahead to a comparison of the youth to the moth which seeks the flame. In general, the effect is to keep in the offing a strong hint that the youth will achieve redemption in battle, and that this will be attained through the domination of feeling over speculation.

2. The religious **metaphor** continues to provide an ironic undercurrent to the narrator's descriptions:

    a. The advancing regiment appears as a "procession of chosen beings" (hence "chosen people").

b. The youth "could have wept in his longings" ("by the waters of Babylon we sat down and wept" - Psalm 137).

c. The youth refers to himself at different moments as "prophet," "seer," and "cowled man."

d. The slain are said to wear "stolen crowns" and "sham robes" (possibly merely the classical laurel and toga, but perhaps suggesting also the crown of martyrdom and the robes of the elect).

The effect of the "religious" **imagery** is still one of wry insinuation that the parallel between religious and military "zeal," "ardency," "ceremony," "worship," and so forth is sound enough, but that it has to be applied consistently, so as to include such things as "bloody sacrifice," "spiritual desolation," and "martyrdom."

THE RED BADGE OF COURAGE

TEXTUAL ANALYSIS

CHAPTERS 12-17

CHAPTER 12

As the chapter opens, the same column of men which had moments before advanced so stoutly and gestured so heroically came flooding out of the woods in retreat. The youth was struck dumb in agony and amazement, and threw aside his "mental pamphlets on the philosophy of the retreated and rules for the guidance of the damned."

Comment

This is perhaps a reference to the unwitting pretentiousness of the titles of philosophical works which promise to teach codes of action from a purely theoretical standpoint (perhaps even specifically to such a title as the twelfth - century Jewish theologian Moses Maimonides' Guide for the Perplexed). If so, the **irony** is twofold, in that no "mental pamphlets" are of any avail in the heat of battle, and also in the fact that the youth has come to see his position not as of one "perplexed," but of one "retreated ... and damned."

The fight, he saw, was lost. The blood-swollen god of war intended to glut itself further. He wanted to cry out, to make a rallying speech, but he could not. Without thinking, he plunged into the midst of them, firing incoherent, unheeded questions at them as they galloped along. Finally he clutched a man by the arm, a man with livid face and rolling eyes, who screamed "Let go me!" and promptly brought his rifle butt down on the youth's head and ran on.

The youth's fingers "turned to paste," and his muscles relaxed. "... He saw the flaming wings of lightning flash before his vision. Suddenly his legs seemed to die. He sank writhing to the ground. He tried to arise. In his efforts against the numbing pain he was like a man wrestling with a creature of the air."

Comment

This passage is rich with significance. First of all, we note that this is Henry's "wound" - what will become his "red badge of courage," and it is inflicted upon him not by the enemy but by one of his own comrades, and a fleeing man at that. Furthermore, the realistic description of the shock and pain (the flash before the eyes, and the rumble in the head) is couched in terms which suggest the suddenness as well as the celestial portentousness of a visionary experience leading to a conversion. Quite specifically, it suggests an analogy with the experience of Saul on the road to Damascus, who fell at a lightning flash to the ground, trembling and astonished, and who, after three days of blindness, was restored to himself as a servant of the Lord. Similarly, the youth's failure to submit to the "religion" of war identifies him as a pagan; after the "lightning flash" and the "rumble of thunder" he falls writhing to the ground, senses dulled, and finally arises and walks "tall soldier fashion" in search of a secluded place to rest.

As he recovers from his swoon, the first thing he notices is a number of officers who are in fact behaving in a most valorous fashion. One, on a "besplashed charger," was making excited motions "with a gauntleted hand." A squadron of cavalry rode up and there was a mighty altercation. The guns suddenly roared out, belching and howling "like brass devils guarding a gate." As he walked on, the "purple darkness was filled with men who lectured and jabbered," with overturned wagons, bodies of horses, and parts of war machines. "It had come to pass" (notice the biblical phrasing) that his wound pained him but little. It had a cool, liquid feeling about it, though his head felt greatly swollen. He was worried, in fact, by his wound's new silence, yet he found opportunity to think about his home, and call up memories of his mother's dishes, the glowing walls of the kitchen, and swimming expeditions with his school chums. Soon, however, he was overtaken by weariness, and slumped along with head bowed until a man with a cheery voice fell in with him, and began to question him, and to talk about his own experiences in battle, concluding that "it was the most mixed up dern thing I ever see." As they passed a wounded officer, the cheery man observed wryly that he would not be so concerned with thoughts of glory when they began to saw off his leg, but added sympathetically, "Poor feller! My brother's got whiskers jest like that." He then embarked on a detailed and matter-of-fact account of the manner in which a friend of his (named "Jack") had met his death that day. All the while that he talked, the man of the cheery voice threaded his way through the mazes of the forest with great keenness until he had found the youth's regiment. With a warm hand clasp, he took his leave, and only then did the youth realize that he had not once caught a glimpse of his face.

SUMMARY

There are two events of central importance in this chapter: the youth receives a head wound from a fleeing comrade; he falls in with a soldier with a "cheery voice," who guides him back to his regiment. In particular:

1. The wounding has three main aspects:

    a. The basic tone of **irony** in *the Red Badge* finds, in this central incident, a strong emphasis since the youth is wounded by a "friend," by the butt of a rifle, and by a fleeing (hence "cowardly") man, while he himself is trying to move toward the front.

    b. In terms of the religious **metaphor** this becomes a "visionary" experience for the youth, attended by lightning (before his eyes) and thunder (within his head), out of which springs his "conversion."

    c. His fall to the ground and consequent efforts to rise "like a babe trying to walk, to his feet" suggests his reduction to a condition of psychological and emotional "infancy" (like *King Lear* on the health) from which point his re-education may begin.

2. The encounter with the "cheery-voiced" man (just after his wound) stands in contrast to his encounter with the "tattered soldier" (just before it). Since he is now "wounded" the cheery soldier accepts him without

> quizzing him about his wounds and parts with a warm handshake. This anticipates the welcome Henry receives (to his surprise) from his comrades in the 304th.

CHAPTER 13

As the youth approached the campfire tended by members of the 304th he thought of hiding in the darkness, but hunger and exhaustion drove him on. Suddenly he was challenged by a shadowy figure with a rifle. It was Wilson (the "loud soldier"), who promptly welcomed Henry with affectionate remarks. The youth thought he had to produce a tale to defend himself against the barbs of his comrades, so he spoke of the terrible fighting he had been in, his separation from the regiment, and his having been "shot" in the head. At this, the corporal (Simpson) stepped up and, recognizing Henry, joined Wilson in exclamations of concern. As Simpson walked off with the youth, Wilson offered him his blanket and his canteen full of coffee.

Once back in the glare of the fire, the corporal had a look at the youth's head, and whistled through his teeth as he probed the "splashed blood and the rare wound." He concluded that the youth had been grazed by a ball, just a "damn' good belt on the head an' nothin' more." Promising to send Wilson to care for him, the corporal went off. As the youth looked around in the dim light, he saw sprawling bodies, and pallid and ghostly visages, looking like men drunk with wine - the "result of some frightful debauch." On the other side of the fire an officer was sleeping, his back against a tree. His body swayed and his jaw hung down; he was the "picture of an exhausted soldier after a feast of war." He had obviously gone to sleep with his sword in his arms, but it had fallen and the brass hilt was in contact with the fire. In the gleam of rose and orange light other sleeping forms could be discerned. "The fire crackled musically." Leaves, silver in color and edged with red, moved softly. Occasionally, in this "low-arched hall," soldiers shifted their positions, sat, blinked at the fire, and lay down once more.

Comment

This scene is clearly meant to parallel that earlier scene (Chapter 7) in which the forest is viewed as a chapel formed by arching boughs, in which the youth comes across the dead soldier, his back propped against a tree. Here, the forest is no longer a "chapel" but a "low-arched hall" (perhaps suggesting the mead hall of Anglo-Saxon warriors).

The youth's reverie was interrupted by the arrival of the loud soldier, who moved about "with the bustling ways of an amateur nurse." "… He fussed around the fire and stirred the sticks to brilliant exertions. He made his patient drink largely from the canteen that contained the coffee. It was to the youth a delicious draught. He tilted his head afar back and held the canteen long to his lips. The cool mixture went caressingly down his blistered throat. Having finished, he sighed with comfortable delight."

Comment

This certainly is one of the most contrived "poetic" passages in the entire book. One notices the continued **alliteration** of f and c, as well as such strained effects as "stirred the sticks" and "long to his lips." The result is a half-ironic, somewhat mocking tone, serving to counterpoint the serious **theme** of "heroic comradeship" which the **imagery** of the chapter (the "low-arched hall," epic-warrior motif) suggests.

Wilson then made a bandage out of a handkerchief and placed it on the youth's head, tying it in a "queer knot" at the back of his neck. To Henry, the cold cloth felt like a woman's tender hand. Wilson's solicitousness, however, began to make him uneasy, and he fumbled with his buttons. The loud soldier then prepared his own blanket as a bed for the youth, who gratefully stretched out on the ground. "He gave a long sigh, snuggled down into his blanket, and in a moment was like his comrades."

Comment

The narrator's final statement is deliberately ambiguous. Henry is like his comrades in the literal sense that he is now wrapped in a blanket and sleeping just as they are. But in another sense the statement is merely a question: Is his "wound" simply a fortuitous occurrence, which has made it possible for him to rejoin his comrades, from whom he does not actually differ with respect to "courage" by any perceptible degree?

SUMMARY

The youth's apprehensions about being jeered at turn out to be groundless. He is received affectionately by Wilson and Simpson, and given the food and rest he needs. Other significant developments:

1. The youth's earlier vision of the forest as a chapel is transformed into one of the forest as a warriors' hall - with a striking parallel between the dead soldier of Chapter 7 and the sleeping officer at Chapter 13.

2. A change has come over Wilson. Not boisterousness but a gentle solicitude seems to be his main characteristic.

> 3. Style - particularly the overly "poetic" touches which are used to describe Wilson's actions - continues to act as a qualification of meaning, giving a touch of **irony** to the narrator's vision of "comradeship."

CHAPTER 14

As the youth awakened from what seemed like a thousand-year sleep, the "quaint light" imparted a corpselike hue to the tangled limbs about him. "His disordered mind interpreted the hall of the forest as a charnel place," but he quickly recognized that this thought was not a fact but a prophecy. In the "heraldic wind of the day," and amidst distant bugles and the rumble of drums the regiment arose. The youth's head felt like a melon, and as Wilson tinkered clumsily at the bandage Henry rebuked him with angry words. Wilson responded in a mollifying tone of voice, and continued to care for Henry's wants; his manner, as the youth began to note, was changed remarkably. He had a "quiet belief in his purposes and abilities.... The youth wondered where had been born these new eyes." Wilson seemed to have "climbed a peak of wisdom" from which he could see his own insignificance.

Comment

The change in Wilson's character is much too abrupt to be realistic, and it proves that *The Red Badge* is not a psychological novel in any ordinary sense. Wilson's change may well be related to the "religious" **metaphor** also, in the sense that he has miraculously conformed to a martial equivalent of the command, "Know thyself"; has "put off the old man and put on the new"; and is no longer "wise in his own conceits."

With some embarrassment Henry pointed out to Wilson the change that had come over him, but Wilson replied casually that he had been a big fool "in those days." Then, after some perfunctory comments about yesterday's battle, the youth reported the fact that Jim Conklin had died, receiving in reply only the noncommittal remark, "Yeh don't say so. Jim Conklin ... poor cuss!" Just then a fracas erupted among some soldiers nearby, and Wilson's efforts to restore only peace achieved for him a challenged to a fight with "a huge soldier" (named Jimmie Rogers). The youth continued to comment on the striking change in his nature, but Wilson shunted aside his remarks, preferring to talk about the dispersion of the regiment on the previous day. "They'd been scattered all over, wanderin' around in th' woods, fightin' with other reg'ments, an' everything. Just like you done." "So?" said the youth (on which noncommittal reply the chapter ends).

SUMMARY

This brief chapter

1. Confirms the change in Wilson's character, and interprets it in terms of the religious metaphor.

2. Establishes beyond question the youth's acceptance by the regiment.

CHAPTER 15

The regiment was just about to march when the youth suddenly remembered the little packet of letters which Wilson (henceforth called usually "his friend") had entrusted to him. He rejoiced in the fact that he possessed a weapon which he could use against Wilson if he should begin to question him about the previous day's battle.

He adopted an air of condescension. His mistakes had been performed in the dark, so he was still a man. Past sufferings were put aside; he had a full stomach and the respect of his fellows. He triumphed in his escape from retribution. He had confidence in himself as a man of experience. In his elation he saw himself as the "chosen of the gods." Even his escape was conducted with dignity, and he felt only scorn for the terror-struck faces of the other fleeing men.

This reverie was interrupted by the voice of Wilson, who sheepishly asked him for the packet of letters. Unable to invent a sufficiently apt Comment on the affair he returned the letters silently, taking credit for his great generosity. The more Wilson blushed in shame, the more Henry felt full of virtues. He became certain that he could entertain audiences at home with romantic tales of his martial accomplishments.

SUMMARY

> The youth's satisfaction over his unchallenged return to the regiment turns to a feeling of superiority and condescension towards Wilson, who has made himself vulnerable with his maudlin speech and the packet of letters. Henry so far forgets his own former acts as to credit himself with a heart that is "strong and stout."

CHAPTER 16

This chapter opens with a style and **imagery** suggestive of the tedium of battle. "A sputtering of musketry was always to be heard. Later, the cannon had entered the dispute. In the fog-filled air their voices made a thudding sound …"

| Comment

Rhythm is occasionally used by Crane to suggest an attitude - at times one of sarcastic exaggeration. Here, the onomatopoeia in the word "sputtering (indicating in its very sound its meaning of "ineffectual, sporadic noise) reinforces the jingling ineffectuality of the rhythm (the opening sentence is also a perfect "fourteener").

x / x / x / x / x / x / x /

"A sputtering of musketry / / was always to be heard."

The curving line of rifle pits looked like a larged furrow. If front was a field filled with deformed stumps. From the woods came a "dull popping" noise, and from the right the sounds of a "terrific fracas." Men "cuddled" behind the embankment; "idle flags were perched" on the hills; the guns were engaged in a "stupendous wrangle." The sound of musketry "growing like a released genie of sound," emphasized the generally disheartened condition of the men. They could not comprehend the idea of defeat. Before the sun had completely obliterated the morning mists, they were retiring through the woods, pursued by the shrill yells of the enemy. The youth, though he realized it might sound unhandsome for him to criticize other men, embarked upon a long denunciation of the commander of his forces. His friend (Wilson) charitably defended the commander, but the youth persisted, demanding loudly, "Don't we do all that men can?" He was dumbfounded at this sentiment as soon as it broke from his lips, but, remaining unchallenged, he recovered his "air of courage," and continued to castigate the mistakes made by "some derned old lunkhead of a general." A sarcastic man asked Fleming if he thought that perhaps he had fought the whole battle himself, and he felt himself pierced by this speech, reduced to an "abject pulp," with quaking legs and a frightened glance. He became more conciliatory and modest.

The rest of the troops were sullen and testy, cursing and muttering as they were pursued by a noise like "the yellings of eager, metallic hounds." As they halted in a clear space, it became apparent that the enemy was about to attack, and there was much growling and swearing. Henry continued his critical murmurings, sharply rebuking an optimistic comment offered by Wilson. A "savage-minded lieutenant" vented his own dissatisfaction by telling them both to shut up. Just as the sun shed its full radiance on the thronged forest a rifle and was followed by a "mighty song of clashes and crashes" which became in turn the rolling thunder of a battle roar. The men, exhausted and hesitant, awaited the shock. Though some flinched and shrank, "they stood as men tied to stakes."

SUMMARY

This chapter is mainly important as showing the youth involved in another kind of mental and emotional turmoil. Formerly introspective, cautious, self-doubting, he has now gone to the other extreme, and, with excessive zeal of the new convert (ironically, since even he is continually aware of his small claim to "courage") criticizes what he conceives to be the shortcomings of those about him.

1. **Imagery**: in their exhaustion the blue soldiers are represented as the object of a "hunt," pursued by "barks" and "hounds."

2. In the jibe of the "sarcastic man" the youth has actually received a second "wound" (it pierces him, weakens his legs, and so forth). This too changes him, making him henceforth a "modest person."

CHAPTER 17

The opening paragraph of this chapter describes the youth as fuming with exasperation at the enemy's refusal to give him time to think - to compose himself. He felt that he had earned the right for contemplative repose.

Comment

We are here reminded that "courage" and "cowardice" have a great deal to do with the opportunity for reflection; Crane is perhaps suggesting the Henry's long period of training and anticipation had conditioned him toward the act of flight.

Yesterday he had hated the universe; today he had "a wild hate for the relentless foe." If they chased him like a kitten he too might develop teeth and claws. At Wilson's calm observation that it seemed they would be driven into the river, the youth cried out savagely. His eyes burned and his teeth were set in a "curlike snarl." The "awkward bandage was still about his head, and upon it, over his wound, there was a spot of dry blood."

Comment

This spot of blood is, in the most literal sense, his "red badge of courage." We are somehow made to imagine that the youth's feeling of terrible hate, his "curlike" rage, and even his very sense of himself as a wounded, tormented, picturesquely desperate figure, are translated directly into the actions Fleming takes, which will later add up to the abstraction of courage.

His fingers twined nervously about his rifle. His rage became a "dark and stormy specter." Suddenly he was again in the midst of a dense wall of smoke, pierced by knifelike fire from the rifles. As in a dream, he sensed that he was pushing back fierce onslaughts of slippery creatures, who skillfully evaded their "beams of crimson." His rifle became an "impotent stick"; losing the habit of balance, he fell heavily; his brain was in chaos. Mechanically he stuffed cartridges into his rifle, aimed, and pulled the trigger. Each time the enemy fell back he went forward, insolently inviting pursuit. "He was so engrossed in his occupation that he was not aware of a lull." He had become such a demon of battle that he kept firing when the enemy was no longer in sight. His astonished comrades had to stop him. As he sprawled on the ground his flesh seemed on fire, and the battle sounds rang in his ears. He seemed drunk with fighting. The lieutenant paid him a magnificent compliment, while others regarded him with awe-struck looks. The friend asked if anything was the matter with him. These things caused the youth to understand that he had become "a barbarian, a beast." He fought "like a pagan who defends his religion." His obstacles had "fallen like paper peaks, and he was now what he called a hero. And he had not been aware of the process. He had slept and, awakening, found himself a knight."

| Comment

Instinct, reflexes, compulsive motions - these have been as responsible for the youth's courageous actions as they were for his earlier flight. The only differences have been in external circumstances, in physiological condition, and in the role which accident had thrust on him - that of the "wounded hero."

The lieutenant cried out deliriously in wild, incomprehensible laughter, unconsciously addressing all martial comments to the youth, while the clamor of musketry still came from the forest. Smoke, arising from it "as from smoldering ruins, went up toward the sun now bright and gay in the blue, enameled sky."

Comment

The forest is no longer cathedral or chapel, the sun no longer blood-red but bright and gay. These impressionistic touches signalize the youth's changed attitude toward war.

SUMMARY

1. The enemy charge, begun in the last chapter, is turned back.

2. The youth becomes a "hero," as a result of:

    a. Lack of time to speculate and ponder.

    b. Sheer exasperation which, coupled with exhaustion, is metamorphosed into blind hatred for the enemy.

    c. The same intense imaginative power that worked towards his earlier flight - except that it now causes him to see himself as a "hunted animal" making a desperate last stand.

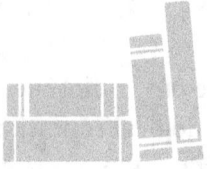

THE RED BADGE OF COURAGE

TEXTUAL ANALYSIS

CHAPTERS 18-24

CHAPTER 18

Though the struggle in the forest increased its din, the "ragged line" of the 304th enjoyed a short lull. A man who had been shot through the body (Jimmie Rogers) cried out bitterly, thrashing about in the grass, and twisting his body into strange positions. The youth's friend, thinking he had seen a stream, went to fetch water. Henry accompanied him, and after a vain search for the stream, during which they spied a burning house, crowds of retreating infantry, and other evidences of the continuing battle, they came upon a mounted general and his staff, who were maneuvering their horses around a wounded man who was crawling on his hands and knees.

Comment

This chapter contains a number of sharp parallels with earlier scenes. Rogers' pained contortions resemble the "hideous hornpipe" danced by Conklin in his death throes; the encounter with the "jangling general and his staff," is like the youth's first encounter with the "jingling general" (in both of which a strategic maneuver is overheard). In this chapter the description is less impressionistic, perhaps suggestive of the youth's growing realism.

Fleming and Wilson lingered nearby, hoping to hear "some great inner historical things," but discovering only that the 304th, which one of the officers compared to "a lot 'a mule drivers," was going to be thrown into the breach to stop the attack - with the likelihood that few of them would get back alive. The youth felt suddenly aged. He was given "new eyes," and the most startling thing to learn was that he was very insignificant. They returned only to meet with a wrathful outburst by the lieutenant for their delay - an outburst which was quickly quelled, however, by the news they brought. Upon hearing it many tightened their belts and hitched up their trousers. The officers, like "critical shepherds," tried to form orderly ranks. None of the others seemed occupied by large thoughts, and Wilson and Fleming mutually nursed their "ironical secret."

SUMMARY

During a lull in the fighting the 304th rests. Wilson and Fleming look for water, and overhear the commanding general's order to send them into the breach. Significant points:

1. Parallels with earlier **episodes** (contortions of wounded soldier, wounded man crawling out of roadway, youth overhearing general's command) underscore Henry's altered imaginative tendencies.

2. The overheard reference to the 304th as "mule drivers" is the ultimate step in the process of de-romanticizing war.

3. The youth for the first time becomes aware of his own insignificance. Couched as it is in terms of his being given "new eyes," this awareness enters into the pattern of religious **metaphor** ("putting off the old man," "dying to self").

CHAPTER 19

An officer rode up, waving his hat, and the line toppled forward. The youth lunged ahead, his face drawn hard, his eyes "fixed in a lurid glare, and his features red and inflamed." The bandage was now a "dingy rag with a spot of blood." Henry headed for a clump of trees, as the regiment, leaving behind a "coherent trail of bodies," seemed to pass into a clearer atmosphere. His senses were heightened; he saw every blade of grass, every curlicue of cloud. The furious rush turned into a frenzy, barbaric cheerings "tuned in strange keys that can arouse the dullard and the stoic." It was a "mad enthusiasm," a "delirium ... heedless and blind to the odds."

Comment

The description of the charge as "frenzy," "delirium," and "enthusiasm" - all terms with **connotations** of religious zeal - leads to one of the rare statements made by the narrator in explanation of courageous actions: "It is a temporary but sublime absence of selfishness. And because it was of this order was the reason, perhaps, why the youth wondered, afterward, what reasons he could have had for being there."

That is, the youth does not realize, when he has time to reflect, that he too was possessed by a frenzy. Finally, their energies slackened and they faltered and hesitated. They were become men again.

Vaguely, the youth felt that he was in some "new and unknown land." Scattered sounds of musketry became a steady roar, and bodies dropped all around. As the regiment dwindled the men appeared dazed - overcome with a "fatal fascination." (This is the crucial moment, which might result either in a charge or a retreat.)

Suddenly, above the sounds of battle, was heard the roar of the young lieutenant. "He strode suddenly forth, his infantile features black with rage." Cursing mightily, he urged them on. Wilson fired a shot at the woods ahead and the men seemed roused to action by it. As they moved ahead jerkily, many could be seen to cower behind trees, as if amazed at the disturbance they had created. "It was the dominant animal failing" (says the narrator, in what is apparently an attempt to define "cowardice") "to remember in the supreme moments the forceful causes of various superficial qualities." The lieutenant continued to bellow profanely, and grabbed the youth by the arm as if he intended to drag him to the fray. With a feeling of "indignation" Henry wrenched free, and followed by Wilson and the lieutenant, galloped ahead. Looking like a "tortured savage" and running like a "madman," the youth closed the gap. "Pulsating saliva stood at the corners of his mouth."

Comment

Objectively regarded, the youth seems in this moment of "courage" most like an animal. Inwardly (and Crane appears to be suggesting an ironic contrast between inner and outer states) he is gripped by the delusion that the flag he was urging on was a "radiant goddess ... a woman, red and white, hating and loving, that called him with the voice of his hopes."

In an instant, the color sergeant flinched and faltered. Henry and his friend together seized the staff from the dead man's hands, and as the corpse swayed one arm swung high "and the curved hand fell with heavy protest on the friend's unheeding shoulder."

SUMMARY

This chapter covers the charge made by the 304th, from the waving of the officer's hat which begins it, through the moment of wavering intentions, to the renewed burst of speed during which Fleming and Wilson seize the flag from the dead color-bearer.

1. From the standpoint of the main **theme**, we find here that much attention is given to the "psychology" of "courage." It is shown variously as:

    a. An enthusiasm producing "a temporary and sublime absence of selfishness," (an "ethical" aspect);

    b. A reversion to savagery and animalism (a "naturalistic" aspect);

c. An ennobling, empowering love centered on the flag as "goddess," (a "religious" aspect).

 2. Parallels with previous motifs and images:

  a. In the vision of the lieutenant's "infantile features black with rage" as he urges them on, the "infancy" figure and the "religious" **metaphor** merge in an ironic version of the biblical text: "A little child shall lead them."

  b. The youth's acquisition of "courage" in succumbing to the romantic symbolism of the flag parallels (also ironically) the part played by the disappointment of romantic expectations in his earlier flight.

CHAPTER 20

In "projectile fashion" the charge spent itself, and the men slowly retreated, contrary to the anguished commands of the officers. One red - bearded officer with a "voice of triple brass" was ordering, "Shoot into 'em, Gawd damn their souls!"

Comment

There is a bit of subtle **irony** in the phrase "triple brass." It is taken from the *Odes of Horace*: "Heart of oak and triple brass lay round the breast of him who first to the savage sea entrusted his frail bark." It is the red-bearded officer's voice, not his heart, which is of "triple brass."

In the melee Wilson and Fleming scuffled briefly over the flag, until the youth roughly pushed his friend away. The regiment continued to retreat under the merciless pelting of bullets, glowering at the officers who harangued them. Stragglers shot irritably at the advancing foes. Among them was the youthful lieutenant, whose wounded arm hung rigidly at his side. The "multiplied pain" seemed only to increase his abilities in swearing. The youth plodded along scowling, wishing he might avenge himself on the officer who had called them "mule drivers." He was possessed by the "rage of the baffled," unable by any amount of cajoling to turn the direction of march. The regiment was a machine run down.

In the smoke and haze the regiment frequently lost its way, and became panic stricken, giving way to hysterical cries, and runnings hither and thither. Amidst the panic the youth stolidly carried the colors, while the officers labored to form the men into a defensive group. The wounded lieutenant stood mutely, his sword held like a cane. He was "like a babe which, having wept its fill, raises its eyes and fixes them upon a distant toy." The youth could see that he was gazing at a body of enemy soldiery, and it seemed to him, too, that their uniforms were "rather gay in effect" and accented with brilliant hues. The clothes seemed new. At the lieutenant's discovery of them, the blue regiment let loose a volley from their "energetic rifles."

| Comment

Even the "infancy" figure is employed here to comment on the instinctive, compulsive nature of actions which later appear to have been "courageous." The lieutenant's brave and self-neglectful stand is interpreted by the narrator as a child's fascination with a colorful bauble, once it has cried its fill.

Angry firings passed back and forth, while the enemy pushed on relentlessly and the youth sat gloomily on the ground, the flag resting between his knees. But the enemy's blows finally weakened, and when the smoke cleared the ground would have been an "empty stage" were it not for a few fantastically twisted corpses on the green. The blue ranks cheered in elation. Events proved that they were not hopelessly outnumbered. They felt a new enthusiasm, new pride, new trust. "And they were men."

SUMMARY

The uncertainty, the vacillation, and the motiveless actions of individuals are here mirrored in the adventitious changes of fortune which the enemy forces undergo. The blue charge spends itself; they retreat in discouragement, a "machine run down"; the gray line then charges, is discovered by an accidental lifting of the smoke (partly because of the newness of their uniforms), and is driven back. (There is some **irony** in the fact that the 304th, without being aware of it, is becoming a "veteran" regiment turning back the charge of an "untried" enemy force.) Various images appear in new and suggestive forms, some of which are:

1. The **"epic" theme** - here in the "red-bearded officer with the voice of triple brass."

2. The "automation" figure - the 304th now a "machine run down."

3. The "infancy" figure - the lieutenant's childlike fascination with "newness" actually helps to turn the charge.

> 4. The "regiment as a broom" **metaphor**, by virtue of the forward - pointing flagstaff, enables the youth to see their possible capture as a broom being swallowed "with bristles forward."

CHAPTER 21

Seeing that they were now free of menacing enemies, the regiment, with anxious backward glances, continued its return to the blue entrenchment. As they approached, they were met by jeers and sarcastic questions, and challenges to fistfights filled the air. The youth "glowered with hate at the mockers," while many of his comrades marched along with heads bowed in shame. Gradually he came to realize the absurdly little distance over which they had traveled, and felt that there was a kind of bitter justice in the taunts of the bronzed veterans, and began to look with disdain on his choking, misty - eyed fellows who strewed the ground. He managed to take some joy, however, in reflecting on his own actions.

His reverie was sharply punctured by the arrival of the officer who had called them "mule drivers," who now rode up savagely to criticize their colonel (MacChesnay) for the awful mess he had made of things. The colonel defended himself lamely, and the irate general rode off. Along the line men reacted with astonishment at the news that they had been reproached, and lapsed into rebellious silence. The youth reacted with a "tranquil philosophy" he had developed, and his friend wore an air of grievance before injustice. They were soothing each other's feelings when several men hurried up to inform them that the colonel had singled Fleming and Wilson out for great praise, saying, "they deserve t' be major generals." With outward modesty, but ill - concealed pleasure, they received these remarks with mutual glances of joy and congratulation. They had a "grateful affection" for the colonel and the lieutenant.

SUMMARY

> The 304th returns to their own line, amid jeers and catcalls. The colonel is sharply rebuked by the general for failing to go the extra hundred feet that would have made it a successful charge. Fleming and Wilson, however, are singled out for bravery, and become suffused with joy and affection for their officer. The chapter is mainly straight narrative, with very little impressionistic description. (The youth has been almost as unaware of the intrepidity of his actions as he was of the timidity which had caused him to flee, and the recognition he receives is almost as accidental as his earlier "wound" in the head.)

CHAPTER 22

At the enemy's next charge the youth felt a supreme self-confidence, which cast its spell over his imaginative grasp of the events before him. Two regiments, a short way off, fought a "blazing" encounter with two of the enemy. A "magnificent brigade" entered a wood, fought, and emerged once more with a jaunty air. "Gruff and maddened" guns "denounced" the enemy. When the four regiments parted the youth could see the two flags "shaking with laughter" amid the remnants of battle. Presently, a solemn but irritating stillness occurred, only to be followed quickly by the renewed din of guns. Desperate rushes of men swelled to and fro. A group of gray forms went forward in "houndlike leaps" and swallowed a mouthful of prisoners, after which a blue wave crashed with thunderous force against a gray obstruction. Vantage points were exchanged like "light toys."

When its time came the 304th charged furiously, ramrods clanging, and arms pounding cartridges into guns. In a brief moment they were smudged with battle dirt once more. The lieutenant was stirred to new exertions in the composition of oaths. The youth, since he bore the colors, remained a spectator of the great drama which confronted him. He was practically oblivious to the exclamations and forced breathings which the scene drew from him. So too with his comrades, for when a gray line came within range they threw up their rifles and fired automatically, without waiting for a command. They fought swiftly and savagely. The youth had resolved not to budge - the "arrows of scorn" which had been loosed at him had generated a fierce hatred within. He conceived of his ultimate revenge taking the form of his torn body lying on the battlefield as a mute reproach to the officer who (in calling them "mule drivers" and "mud diggers") had "dubbed him wrongly." As he watched, the orderly sergeant of the company was shot through the cheeks and ran screaming to the rear, his mouth a "pulsing mass of blood and teeth." Others, too, fell, their bodies twisted into fantastic shapes. He saw Wilson, who now appeared as a "vehement young man, powder-smeared and frowzled." The lieutenant was still cursing, but with the air of a man who was "using up his last box of oaths." The fire of the regiment was beginning to wane.

SUMMARY

Here we see the youth lost in a kind of euphoria, looking at the battle as a spectator. The main line of the enemy makes occasional forays out from behind the protection of a fence, but finally settles down behind it.

1. From the standpoint of the youth's psychological state, this is a lull before the stormy charge he will make in the following chapter.

2. As for his comrades, their status as "veteran troops" becomes increasingly clear, with the growing automatism they gain.

CHAPTER 23

The colonel appeared on the run, and calling for a charge. The youth saw, too, that to remain where they were was certain death. He expected that his comrades would have to be driven to the attack, but was surprised to see that they were eager for the rush. There follows one of the most memorable passages in the book: "... At the yelled word of command the soldiers sprang forward in eager leaps. There was new and unexpected force in the movement of the regiment. A knowledge of its faded and jaded condition made the charge appear like a paroxysm, a display of the strength that comes before a final feebleness. The men scampered in insane fever of haste, racing as if to achieve a sudden success before an exhilarating fluid should leave them."

Comment

It is significant that the regiment, collectively at their most "courageous" moment, should be depicted as being in the grip of paroxysm - an involuntary, reflexive action. The narrator also refers to it shortly as "an enthusiasm of unselfishness," a "state of frenzy," and a "sublime recklessness," and notes that the youth himself "felt the daring spirit of a savage religion-mad," and was "shaken and dazzled by the tension of thought and muscle." Clearly, this is Crane's way of equating bravery with the compulsive responses of an orgiastic frenzy, and he emphasizes its sublogical character by remarking that in all of this "there was no obvious questioning, nor figurings, nor diagrams."

As the blue wave rolled on many of the enemy turned and ran, except for one "obdurate group" entrenched behind a fence. Suddenly, they clashed, the cheers of the men in blue turning to yells or wrath as they sought the foe. The youth regarded the enemy flag as a "craved treasure of mythology" and leaped at the rival color bearer, who was mortally wounded. Wilson preceded him, however, and wrenched the flag free, amid wild clamorings of cheers.

When the smoke cleared, four of the enemy were seen to have been captured. One, with a superficial foot wound, was cursing heartily; another - a boy in years - took his plight calmly and good-naturedly; a third reacted with a morose stoicism; and the fourth seemed lost in an abject and profound shame over his captivity. Amid celebration, the youth and his friend sat congratulating each other.

SUMMARY

1. This chapter contains the **climax** of the novel, both from the standpoint of action (the enemy position is finally overwhelmed, and prisoners are taken) and of **theme** (the regiment and the youth resolve the problem of "courage" in an orgiastic plunge into the midst of the enemy).

2. In addition, a number of image patterns achieve their final statement. Two examples:

    a. "Religious" **metaphor** - the youth finally feels himself "capable of profound sacrifices, a tremendous death."

    b. The pagan "**epic**" motif - the enemy flag, now viewed as a "craved treasure of mythology" (like the Golden Fleece) is seized by Wilson and Fleming.

3. There is a fine **irony** in the fact that the prisoners are mirrors of the very attitudes displayed by the soldiers in blue.

CHAPTER 24

As the roarings ceased, the youth felt almost a regret at their passing. In a short time the regiment received orders to move, and trampled slowly back over the same ground. Finally, the youth understood that it was all over, though it took some time for his mind to cast off its "battleful ways." Like a spectator watching a procession of memory he reviewed his performances, and was gleeful at the fact that his public deeds "were paraded in great and shining memory." Taking great pleasure in his reflections, "he saw that he was good."

Comment

This clearly echoes Genesis (1:31): "And God saw everything that he had made, and, behold, it was very good." It is the youth's moment of supreme inflation, during which he contemplates his accomplishments from a godlike eminence, ignoring entirely both their insubstantiality and his own passive role.

This reverie was marred only by the ghost of his first flight, and the image of the tattered soldier whom he had deserted in the field (and the possibility that he might have been detected). Giving vent to a small outcry, he was accosted by his friend Wilson, but replied merely with a string of crimson oaths. For a time all elation was gone from him, yet he gradually found the strength to put his sin at a distance. He could now "look back upon the brass and bombast of his earlier gospels and see them truly." In despising them, he gained assurance, and felt that, after all, he was a man.

Though others muttered as they slogged along in the rain, the youth smiled, having rid himself of the "red sickness of battle." The sun's golden rays pierced through the leaden rain clouds.

SUMMARY

The final chapter shows the blue soldiers turning, after their success, back to the rear. The youth is first seen to be elated with his performance, then wretchedly fearful of exposure, and finally calm and optimistic in the assurance of his achieved manhood.

Other details:

1. The "religious **metaphor**" appears once in an ironic version (the youth's "godlike" surveyal of his accomplishments), and once in a serious version (Henry's rejection of his "earlier gospels" of vanity).

2. This final use of the religious motif, which amounts to a Pauline "putting on of the new man," merges with the pattern of primitive anthropological **imagery** in the suggestion that battle has also been for the youth his rite de passage (passage from youth to manhood).

3. The final element of nature **imagery** supports both of the above details. The wretched sky, filled with rain clouds, and the muddy trough of the road, give way to a vision of fresh meadows and cool brooks dominated by the golden sun.

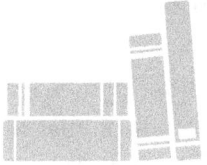

THE RED BADGE OF COURAGE

CHARACTER ANALYSES

"THE YOUTH" (HENRY FLEMING)

In one sense the entire book is a character analysis of Henry Fleming, and it seems pointless to try to condense Crane's own elaborately conceived fiction. But we do learn a number of things about the youth initially. He is sensitive, introspective, and romantic, and above all eager to test his own inner depths. From one point of view Henry's progress through the book amounts to a series of shocking contrasts between the glorified images of heroic deeds his imagination conjures up and the grim realities of battle, death, and decay. His initial ignorance of his own limits causes Fleming to vacillate between diffidence and braggadocio, as he speculates about his possible reactions under fire; at first, of course, he flees, but ultimately he comes to terms with himself and evolves into a normal (perhaps even a heroic) "veteran." With an extraordinarily complicated narrative **irony**, Crane, by shifting back and forth from the viewpoint of the youth himself to that of a critical and omniscient observer, presents a parade of persons and events which objectify in a more or less impressionistic fashion the youth's quest for self-knowledge and a more perfect integration of thought, feeling, and action. Jim

Conklin's example, the tattered man's exhortations, the cheery man's firm guidance, the kindly ministrations of Wilson - all mark periods in Fleming's psychological growth. As Crane presents it, the **climax** of the process is the charge, in the course of which Henry's acquired ethical feeling of brotherhood, the surge of natural impulse, and a quasi-religious spark of enthusiasm blend to produce what the world calls "heroism."

THE "TALL SOLDIER" (JIM CONKLIN)

We encounter Conklin three times. He first appears as a somewhat opinionated - almost overbearing - individual, one whom the very prospect of war has transformed from an unimpressive plodder into a self-assured warrior. On his second appearance the near approach to battle seems to have infused into him a professional coolness and proficiency. Conklin's third (and last) appearance is as the "spectral soldier" in the line of wounded men retreating to the rear. Here he has become a symbol of an absolute yielding to the pressures of combat - a sacrifice to the gods of war (with a possible resemblance of some sort to Christ, the sacrificial Victim).

THE "LOUD SOLDIER" (WILSON)

Wilson is a very simple character, but one who undergoes a remarkable transformation. Only in the beginning, before combat, is he the "loud soldier," a querulous, argumentative fellow, given to peremptory challenges and sarcastic comments. As the 304th approaches the line of fire, however, he comes to Henry with the lugubrious prediction that this is to be his first and last battle. When they next meet, after Fleming's retreat and the blow on the head, he has been utterly changed from his former attitudes, and is a gentle and humble companion. Thereafter he is referred to by Crane as "the friend," and seems to stand as an emblem of the kind of personal "reformation" war is capable of bringing about.

THE "YOUNG LIEUTENANT" (HASBROUCK)

Hasbrouck is an example of the man who can perform heroically without the agony of self-questioning. He is a natural leader - brave, blunt, and harsh when necessary, but respected for his abilities and accomplishments. His youth and his uncomplicated approach to the question of "bravery" make him a foil to Fleming.

THE "TATTERED MAN"

This unnamed soldier is one of Crane's most mysterious creations. He exemplifies an attitude - one of absolute, naive simplicity - which, by being the very epitome of ingenuousness, represents an unwitting threat to the dissembler.

THE "CHEERY MAN"

Like the "tattered man" he is without a name, and, for the youth, without a face. He seems to Henry to possess a "magic wand" by which he threads his way through the mysterious darkness, and yet his conversation is most prosaic and his achievements most practical - he returns the youth to his comrades.

"HE OF THE INJURED FINGERS" (BILL SMITHERS)

Smithers is by no means a major character but he stands as a curious antithesis to Henry. He too has a spurious wound, but it enables him to malinger his way through the battle, while a strain of inventive comedy helps him to save face.

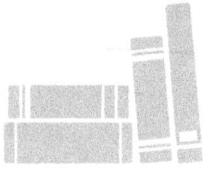

THE RED BADGE OF COURAGE

CRITICAL COMMENTARY

The Red Badge of Courage is now universally recognized as a masterpiece, although when it first appeared in book form in 1896 (two months later in England than in the United States) it provoked mixed reactions. The English critics, in fact, brought it to the attention of the American public, which had generally ignored it. Those early readers who approved saw in it a "true and complete picture of war," a book which "thrusts aside romantic machinery" in favor of dramatic action and photographic revelation. Its critics attacked it for what they considered its utter lack of literary form - its "absurd similes," "bad grammar," and "violent straining after effect." Edward Garnett, however, praised its "perfect mastery of form," and Conrad, who had known Crane, said in 1926 that *The Red Badge of Courage* was a "spontaneous piece of work which seems to spurt and flow like a tapped stream from the depths of the writer's being," and he found it "virile and full of gentle sympathy" while it was happily marred by no "declamatory sentiments." Throughout the first four decades of the century the book was variously praised and condemned for its naturalism or "animalism," its **realism** and its extraordinary style. V. S. Pritchett, writing in 1946, may be said to represent the prevailing opinion when he declares that Crane's "verisimilitude," his grasp of "human feelings," and his "dramatic scenes and portraits" give *The Red Badge of Courage* a place in the literature of war.

CRITICISM IN THE 1940S

It is only in the forties that serious literary analysis of the book begins. It had of course long been recognized that novels such as Zola's *La Debacle* and Tolstoy's *Sevastopol* and *War and Peace* had had some influence on Crane, and that he had made use of Battles and Leaders of the Civil War (which had first appeared serially in the *Century Magazine*) as well as accounts of particular campaigns; his brother William, for one thing, was an expert on the strategy of the Battle of Chancellorsville, and there are many parallels with this battle to be found in *The Red Badge*. But scholars like Pratt, Webster, Osborn, and Stallman began to call attention to the possible role played by less significant factors, like Crane's personal acquaintance with General Van Petten, an instructor at Claverack College, who might have provided him with a first-hand account of the Battle of Antietam. Crane may also have derived some less important conceptions from Civil War potboilers like Hinman's *Corporal Si Klegg* or Kirkland's *The Captain of Company K*. Although Crane himself acknowledged an early influence by Kipling's novels, it was S. C. Osborn who pointed out that the famous "red wafer" image at the close of Chapter 9 probably had its source in Kipling's *The Light That Failed*, and who thereby inaugurated a discussion (maintained chiefly by R. W. Stallman) about the meaning of this image. The "wafer" may be a wax sealing wafer or it may be, as Stallman suggests, an **allusion** to the Christian communion wafer, but it lies at the center of the controversy concerning the alleged Christian symbolism of the novel.

CRITICISM IN THE 1950S

Discussions of the structure and total meaning of the novel date from about 1950. John Schroeder believes that Crane has not achieved a successful accommodation of antithetical elements: "War as man-made blasphemy" is not "distinguishable from nature's pattern of serene wisdom"; and he feels that the "putting off of the Old Man [by the youth] ... is largely a matter of accident." R. W. Stallman, on the other hand, asserts that a consistent, meaningful pattern unifies the story. *The Red Badge* "is about the self - combat of a youth who fears and stubbornly resists change and spiritual growth.... Henry's regeneration is brought about by the death of Jim Conklin." Psychological and mythic criticism of a book whose action centers mainly about a "wound" was perhaps inevitable, and Maxwell Geismar (1953) explains that "Fleming's shame at his psychic wound ... led him to yearn for the physical wound." The basic pattern of the narrative conforms to that of "acceptance after a trial by ordeal." Geismar further sees this as all a reflection of Crane's own "psychic wound," declaring that "much of Crane's career was spent in the attempt to validate the imaginary experience in *The Red Badge of Courage* by the test of battle itself." In a similar vein, J. E. Hart concludes that *The Red Badge* is about the making of a "hero" (in the mythical sense). Noting that Henry atones for his guilt with blood and then feasts communally with his comrades, Hart decides that through atonement and rebirth (Henry's awakening from a "thousand years' sleep") he has become a member of the tribal unit. "Following the general pattern of myth ... Crane has shown how the moral and spiritual strength of the individual springs from the group."

CONVENTIONAL CONCLUSION

A more conventional conclusion has been reached by M. Solomon, who regards Crane's novel as a "study in the meaning of social responsibility and freedom," interpreting the youth's flight as an act of blind defiance of authority and his return as a "submission to arbitrary power and to the military." Solomon finds that the deepest patriotism of the novel is to be discovered in Crane's "devotion to and confidence in the common people." A far greater degree of ironic detachment is imputed to the author by Charles C. Walcutt, who observes that the terms Crane employs "suggest [that war is] a solemn farce or a cosmic and irresponsible game." Henry, he believes, "has never been able to evaluate his conduct…. The whole business is made of pretense and delusion."

RECENT POLEMICS

Recent statements have occasionally been polemical. Philip Rahv (in 1956) attacked the views of Stallman and his supporters, claiming that they misappropriated techniques of poetic analysis in reading Crane's novel. Rahv contended that Stallman's "Christian allegorical" reading was absurd, and that such interpretations as that of taking Jim Conklin's initials to be a reference to Jesus Christ reduce criticism to a cabalistic hunt for clues. Stanley Greenfield takes earlier critics to task for misreading the text and takes the position that Crane's **irony** "neatly balances two major views of human life … ethical motivation and behavior versus deterministic and naturalistic actions." Colvert also sees a double point of view in the story, but adapts his position to the "redemption" theory. "The structure of the novel," he asserts, "is characteristically a series of loosely related ironic **episodes** built up in the contrast between two points of view toward reality." These two viewpoints are a subjective illusory one, and the objective "long view" of the narrator. "Henry is redeemed by a successful adjustment of his point of view."

RECENT CRITICISM

Two fairly recent evaluations of *The Red Badge* may serve to epitomize the contradictory responses Crane's story continues to evoke. Norman Friedman is convinced that "Fleming undergoes no change of character whatsoever ... the change which he does undergo [being] one of thought," while James T. Cox sees in the book the idea "that the selfless behavior of heroism paradoxically emerges only from the grossest, most infantile, animalistic, fiery hatred born of the vanity of egocentrism." It does not seem likely, in view of such discrepancies of viewpoint, that agreement about total meaning of *The Red Badge of Courage* is soon to be reached.

THE RED BADGE OF COURAGE

ESSAY QUESTIONS AND ANSWERS

Question: In what respects may Crane's style be said to be "poetic?"

Answer: One might make a very rough distinction between narrative fiction and poetry by indicating that the former emphasizes the larger elements of plot, characterization, and action whereas the latter presents its meaning through patterns for **imagery**, rhythm, **diction**, and figurative language. In poetry the emphasis is on the word and the image - in the novel it is on **episode** and character relationship and development. It seems clear, however, that Crane relies heavily on poetic techniques to achieve his meaning. The personification of the forces and the engines of war, and the tendency to represent human intentions and manmade objects as parts of an organismal process are basic features of Crane's style, helping to express his ironic and skeptical viewpoint. He uses color to symbolizes attitudes and moods, and rhythm to suggest psychological states or the pace of action. Crane's diction (at times markedly Biblical) amounts to a general pattern of allusion, defining war as a kind of sacrilege. All these factors indicate that any definition of *The Red Badge* as a novel should be broad enough to include its use of poetic techniques.

THE RED BADGE OF COURAGE

Question: How is the narrator's point of view related to the total meaning of the book?

Answer: The narrator's point of view consists of a complicated sort of **irony** towards his chief character, Henry Fleming, and his subject, war. He allows himself a limited access into the youth's mind, sufficient to make clear Henry's initial and continuing tendency to romanticize sordid realities, but he continually retreats to a more objective and external ground when, for example, he wishes to comment ironically on the indifference which Nature displays towards man's pretentious efforts to outstrip her limitations. The narrator is simultaneously critical of society's stupid blasphemies against the order of nature, and of nature itself, which places such unreasonable obstacles in its way. The individual too, to the extent that he strives in isolation towards ego fulfillment, appears in an ironic light. In short, the point of view is fundamentally ambiguous, critical and sympathetic in an imponderable blend.

Question: What is the significance of the description of the four prisoners taken by the soldiers in blue?

Answer: For one thing, the very fact that "the enemy" is now visualized as a mere group of men - very prosaic and practically indistinguishable from their captors - signalizes the end of any possibility of conceiving of the enemy as "dragons" or "monsters." More profoundly, perhaps, the capture of these men suggests that Fleming has even gone beyond identification with the members of his own regiment to identification with the "enemy," hence achieving status in a human totality. For their individualizing traits, while they repeat characteristics formerly noted in Henry's comrades, also serve as emblems of his own questing personality. One nurses a "superficial wound"; another is a boy with "bright and keen eyes"; a third is morose and stoical;

the fourth is lost in abject shame. In capturing and comprehending them, Henry comes to further knowledge of himself.

Question: Explain the symbolic interpretation which may be placed upon the youth's encounter with the corpse in Chapter 7.

Answer: The following three points may suggest the way to a more complete analysis:

   a. In the "religious half light" of the "chapel" made by arching boughs, the corpse with its back against a "columnlike tree" becomes a sacrifice to the gods of war (who must also be identified to some extent with nature herself).

   b. The corpse's change of colors - to a "melancholy green," a "dull hue," and "appalling yellow," and "gray" - points almost to an autumnal decline, suggesting that the victims of war blend inevitably into the cyclical progress of the seasons.

   c. The look which the youth exchanges with the corpse indicates their essential kinship. He may flee from a particular occasion of battle, but the process of nature identified in this scene is a heritage that he cannot escape.

Question: Discuss the "realistic" aspects of Crane's method of introducing his readers to new characters and new scenes.

Answer: Like Conrad, particularly in Lord Jim, Crane wants to provide his reader with a sense of the rush and flux and events - to re-create for him the air of confusion and disconnectedness which surround our apprehension of violent affairs in real life.

In *The Red Badge* we do not find, as we do in Lord Jim, confusing shifts of time attributable to the idiosyncrasies of memory of a narrator whose own evaluation of events controls his selection and ordering of them, but we do notice on the part of the narrator a refusal to make clear expository comments on the action. For example, we learn in Chapter 2 that a man who has fallen down during the march has had his fingers stepped on, but he is identified only as "he of the injured fingers." At the beginning of Chapter 4 we overhear a snatch of conversation about the same incident, in which we learn that the soldier's name is Bill, and that he is believed to have shown considerable pluck in refusing to allow a doctor to amputate his three crushed fingers. In Chapter 6 another bit of conversation introduces a man who complains about the fighting and wishes that "Bill Smithers had trod on my hand insteader me treddin' on his'n," and we are made aware of the possibility that Smithers' minor injury may have given him a fortunate excuse for malingering and avoiding real danger (a possibility that receives further confirmation in Chapter 24). The reader only gradually learns the identity of Bill Smithers, even while he is made to modify in succession his attitudes toward Bill, just as this experience comes to us in real life. Withal, there is a sense of connectedness and continuity underlying the effect of confusion and of groping efforts to learn the details of the surrounding situation.

Question: Does Henry Fleming undergo a change of character in the course of the novel?

Answer: There are basically three points of view on this question.

- a. Some critics believe that Henry is "redeemed" from his cowardice, perhaps by the example of the "sacrificial" death of Jim Conklin and the new humility of Wilson - that he not only becomes heroic in battle but undergoes a complete reversal of personality, putting aside his youthful vanity and braggadocio and achieving the reasoned assurance of manhood.

b. Others believe that Fleming's "reform" is merely specious, and his self-knowledge a delusion-that once removed from the excitement and glamor of the battlefield he will return to his shallow attitudes. This, so it is argued, is indicated by the youth's sanguine expectations of a long life of peace as he marches away from the battle at the book's end.

c. A third group rejects both the "religious reformation" notion as well as the theory that Henry has not developed at all, and suggest instead that there is indeed a growth in Henry's attitude and insight, but that it occurs purely on the natural level of a deepening psychological awareness and ability to evaluate experience. This view in its general form rejects any symbolic reading of *The Red Badge*.

Actually, Crane's complicated **irony** and the lack of an unambiguous narrative and expository voice make it extremely difficult to deduce Crane's meaning. Growth there seems to be - though our interpretation of the form it takes may have to await further critical evaluation.

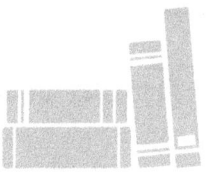

THE RED BADGE OF COURAGE

TOPICS FOR RESEARCH AND CRITICAL ANALYSIS

CRANE'S STYLE

a. Define the stylistic elements which identify a work as realistic, romantic, or impressionistic. To what extent are these details present in the verbal patterns of *The Red Badge of Courage*?

b. From the standpoint of style - particularly the use of rhythm and **imagery** - what distinguishes prose from poetry? To what extent can the writer of fiction use the devices of poetry? When is the literary critic justified in applying the techniques of poetic criticism to the novel? In this connection consider the disagreement between Stallman and Rahv, and try to settle the issue in your own mind.

c. What part is played by literary **allusion** in Crane's style? How do echoes of Biblical phrasing, or of stereotyped romantic formulas enter into the pattern of irony?

THE RED BADGE AS A PICTURE OF WAR

a. Compare Crane's book with one of its better known predecessors - Zola's *La Debacle*, for instance, or Tolstoy's *Sevastopol*. Which impresses you as more real - true to the physical actualities of battle and to the psychological reactions of a youth in combat?

b. Compare *The Red Badge* with one or more novels of the First or Second World Wars - Hemingway's *A Farewell to Arms*, for example, or Mailer's *The Naked and the Dead*. In what respects do the later authors surpass Crane? In what ways does he remain superior?

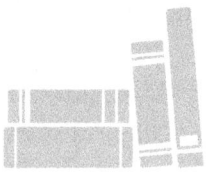

THE RED BADGE OF COURAGE

GUIDE TO FURTHER STUDY

Read Walt Whitman's *Drum Taps* with an eye to scenes resembling those in *The Red Badge* ("Bivouac on a Mountain Side," perhaps, or "An Army Corps on the March"). Analyze comparable scenes from the standpoint of poetic technique and effectiveness.

As one method of defining more exactly Crane's sort of "naturalism" make a comparison of the youth's flight from battle with that of Pepe in John Steinbeck's short story entitled "Flight."

Compare the **episode** in which Fleming comes upon the dead soldier in the forest with the incident in William Golding's *Lord of the Flies* in which the boys discover the dead pilot. In what respects does Crane's sort of symbolism resemble (and in what ways differ from) Golding's? This might be part of a more lengthy comparison between Crane and Golding, perhaps based on the anthropological or mythic substratum to the stories.

There are a number of scenes in *The Red Badge* which do not immediately suggest their relationship to the major **theme** of the book. Some of them are:

a. Henry's memory of the light-haired and dark-haired girls who had reacted so differently to his farewell (Chapter 1).

b. The fat soldier's attempt to steal a horse from a young girl (Chapter 2).

c. The youth's memory of his childish thrill at the spring arrival of the circus parade - in particular the image of the "old fellow who used to sit upon a cracker box in front of the store and feign to despise such exhibitions" (Chapter 5). Consider the possible function these **episodes** have in the total structure of the novel. Do they find parallels or antitheses in other incidents?

It has been observed that characters like Jim Conklin, the "tattered soldier," and the "cheery soldier" are not types of human beings but very particular, concretely functioning plot elements.

a. With what success can one, by regarding Crane's battle as a metaphor for human life in its wider aspects, interpret these characters in a typological way? On such a reading, what would be the meaning of the "tattered soldier"? the "man with the cheery voice"? the "tall soldier" (Jim Conklin)? "He of the injured fingers" (Bill Smithers)?

b. It is perhaps possible to conceive of these characters as projections of aspects of Henry Fleming's own character? If so, why do they appear when they do, and how are their actions particularly suited to the stage at which the youth has arrived in his quest for self-knowledge?

Why does Crane (in Chapter 23) describe the four prisoners in such detail? In what ways do they resemble soldiers of the blue army described earlier?

Analyze the total structure of the novel with respect to one or more of the following elements:

a. **Imagery** - colors, animal metaphors, aspects of nature;

b. **Action** - the consistency of time sequences, charges and retreats, and marches (does Crane give evidence of having had a carefully elaborated temporal and geographical pattern always in view?);

c. **Psychology** - the relationship between Fleming's character as it is presented in the more or less expository passages, and his actions. Note also the relationship between the force of external circumstances (lack of food, confusion, the blow on the head, the "examples" the youth is confronted by) and his actions and decisions.

Is there any growth in Henry Fleming's character? If so, how, and to what extent?

Consider the philosophical issues raised by the book.

a. Is it a deterministic novel?

b. What is man's relationship to nature, and the extent of the role played by natural instinct in human conduct as Crane presents it?

c. What is Crane's attitude toward formal religious ritual, and toward received ethical standards, as this is revealed in his novel?

The Red Badge of Courage in the context of Crane's work as a whole: Read Crane's poetry, his letters, or his other short fiction, and decide how *The Red Badge* conforms to the attitudes found therein. Do his opinion and his vision of human life change from work to work?

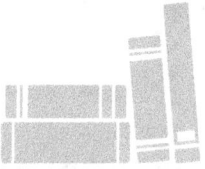

BIBLIOGRAPHY

EDITIONS

The Work of Stephen Crane, ed. Wilson Follett, 12 vols., New York, 1925–27.

Stephen Crane: An Omnibus, ed. Robert W. Stallman, New York, 1952.

Stephen Crane: Stories and Tales, ed. Robert W. Stallman, New York (Vintage Books), 1955.

The Red Badge of Courage, ed. with an introduction by Robert W. Stallman, New York, 1951.

Stephen Crane: The Red Badge of Courage and Other Stories, introduction by V. S. Pritchett, London, 1960.

BIOGRAPHY

Thomas Beer, *Stephen Crane: A Study in American Letters*, New York, 1923.

John Berryman, *Stephen Crane*, New York, 1950.

Edwin H. Cady, *Stephen Crane*, New York, 1962.

Hamlin Garland, "Stephen Crane as I Knew Him," *Yale Review*, III (1914), 494–506.

BIBLIOGRAPHY

Ames W. Williams and Vincent Starrett, *Stephen Crane: A Bibliography*, Glendale, Calif., 1948.

Robert N. Hudspeth, ed., "A Bibliography of Stephen Crane Scholarship: 1893–1962," (*Thoth*, IV (1963), 30–58.

COLLECTIONS OF CRITICISM

The Red Badge of Courage: An Annotated Text, Backgrounds and Sources, Essays in Criticism, ed. S. Bradley, R. C. Beatty, and E. H. Long, New York, 1962.

Stephen Crane's The Red Badge of Courage: Text and Criticism, ed. R. Lettis, R. F. McDonnell, and W. E. Morris, New York, 1960.

SELECTED SCHOLARLY AND CRITICAL STUDIES

Joseph Conrad, "His War Book: A Preface to Stephen Crane's *The Red Badge of Courage*," in *Last Essays*, London, 1926.

Robert W. Stallman, "Stephen Crane: A Revaluation," *Critiques and Essays on Modern Fiction*, ed. John Aldridge, New York, 1952.

John E. Hart, "The Red Badge of Courage as Myth and Symbol," *University of Kansas City Review*, XIX (1953).

Isaac Rosenfeld, "Stephen Crane as Symbolist," *Kenyon Review*, XV (1953).

Philip Rahv, "Fiction and the Criticism of Fiction," *Kenyon Review*, XVIII (1956).

Robert W. Stallman, "Fiction and Its Critics: A Reply to Mr. Rahv," *Kenyon Review*, XIX (1957).

Bernard Weisberger, "The Red Badge of Courage," in *Twelve Original Essays on Great American Novels*, ed. Charles Shapiro, Detroit, 1958.

Stanley B. Greenfield, "The Unmistakable Stephen Crane," *PMLA*, LXXIII (1958).

James T. Cox, "The **Imagery** of *The Red Badge of Courage*," *Modern Fiction Studies* (1959).

Harold R. Hungerford, "'That Was at Chancellorsville': The Factual Framework of *The Red Badge of Courage*," *American Literature*, XXXIV (1963).

www.ingramcontent.com/pod-product-compliance
Lightning Source LLC
LaVergne TN
LVHW012058070526
838200LV00070BA/2970